The Friendship Formula

SARAVANAN M S

notionpress.com

INDIA · SINGAPORE · MALAYSIA

CONTENTS

Chapter I
THE JOY OF FRIENDSHIP

Friendship isn't a big thing; it's a million little things

– Paulo Coelho

The Earth and the sky were friends. One day, when the Earth saw the sky turning gloomy and its clouds becoming dark out of sadness, it smiled a little and consoled him, saying, "Don't worry, my dear, pour your tears all over me. I will lock them in."

Friends are the place of solace. Life can give us a hundred reasons to worry, but friends can give us a thousand reasons to smile. The time we spend with our friends is always memorable. We cherish those times until we meet them again. Friendship thus gives happiness and wonderful memories to cherish and value in our lives.

C. S. Lewis said, "Friendship is born at the moment when one man says to another, 'What! You too? I thought I was the only one!'"

Friendship is a bond between people that connects them and lets them share each other's feelings and thoughts. It is a close association with someone with whom you can tell anything, care for them, respect, admire, and love them. Basically, friendship is a long-term relationship of mutual affection and support.

To make your stressful and frenzied life comparatively less stressful, you need friends. When you are feeling low, friends make you burst into laughter. When you accomplish something, friends will celebrate your win with you. No matter how your other relationships make you feel, the beautiful bonding called friendship will always be there to enrich your life significantly.

A friend is an absolutely essential connection to maintain throughout a lifetime. According to the Huffington Post, lack of friendship has been associated with higher chances of premature death than obesity. Friendships are required not only for mental health but for longevity. To enjoy a happier, healthier, and more productive life, friendships are essential, says a PLoS Medicine meta-analysis review of 148 studies with over 300,000 people. Thus, friendship must be considered a crucial relationship among people.

We, humans, are social by nature. Since the evolutionary time, people who were hunters and gatherers relied heavily on others for survival. Having people around with whom one can cooperate increases the chances of survival. When hunters got injured, their friends provided and supported them until they got back on their feet. This kind of help and support continued in the later stages of human evolution when our ancestors started cultivation. Effective cooperation of individuals was required in cultivation, enabling people to establish connections and friendships.

As it is said, "A friend in need is a friend indeed." People form friendships mainly to have mutual support and help. However, different people may have distinct requirements for friendship according to their preferences. One may call someone a friend within minutes of meeting them, while for others, it may take days and weeks to become friends with someone. Some have friends for support and encouragement, while some people remain friends only for fun. There is no absolute definition of what constitutes a friendship. But there are some common traits of a friendship. They are:

- Feelings of love and respect.

- Feelings of admiration and appreciation.

- Loyalty and commitment,

- Communication.

- Shared interests, opinions, beliefs, or hobbies.

- Mutual trust, concern, and compassion.

In any relationship, love is natural and essential. In a friendship, love means being there for a friend in any circumstance. Love is listening to our friend's problems and helping them to find a perfect solution to those problems. It is the care and concern we have for each other. Love comes with the utmost respect for the person. Love and respect are the 2 sides of the same coin. Love ties into respect, which is another important part of true friendship.

Respect in any relationship is not given but earned. When friends show how much they love and care for each other, respect forms between them, and such love with respect gives each other their space to be themselves. The love we have for our friends respect them for who they are. There will be mutual respect for each other's opinions, beliefs, and ideologies in a true friendship.

However, setting boundaries is also important in a friendship. It may sound like erecting a wall between friends, but boundaries actually can help outline how you will navigate your friendship in a way that takes both people's needs and desires into account. Conveying clearly about your free time to hang out and the activities that you are comfortable with or not comfortable with helps you to make your friends understand who you are and what you are expecting from their friendship.

Sometimes, such scenarios tend to bring misunderstandings between friends. One may want to hang out in a place where the other does not feel comfortable. In such circumstances, communicating our feelings helps. The depth of intimacy occurs in a friendship only when there is perfect communication.

The most important part of any healthy friendship or relationship is the ability to talk and listen to one another. Communication is essential for a friendship to survive and thrive. To build a healthy friendship, friends should be able to communicate with each other effectively because a friendship can flourish only when both people feel comfortable around each other. If one always feels like walking on eggshells, one cannot enjoy the benefits of true friendship.

Also, there has to be the idea of mutuality in a friendship. In friendship, no one is superior, and no one is inferior to the other. Such power dynamics are not entertained in friendships. Both friends must feel at ease in the presence of one another.

To feel at ease, they must appreciate each other's effort in maintaining their relationship. Any relationship will get weakened without proper acknowledgement or appreciation. Friends need to be appreciated in a way that will make them truly feel appreciated. By making them a priority in our life, we can show them they are loved, and their well-being is important to us. Also, having regular contact with them makes them feel appreciated. By calling them over the phone or physically spending time with them, we can show them how important they are. While any friendship can ebb and flow over time, some consistent sense of forwarding momentum is necessary to keep it intact. In other words, there needs to be clear expectations for the level of communication and connection you'll have with a friend, whether that means texting every day, calling every week, or getting together for a longer catch-up once a month. Our friends deserve our time, presence, and companionship, and we are perfectly suited to be the shoulder they may need to lean on in times of distress and despair.

One of the most important qualities a friend can have is loyalty. The one who is loyal is the one who is reliable. We can trust such a person because they will always have our back. Loyalty is what sets true friends apart from the rest of the pack. Loyalty and commitment go hand in hand. Commitment to friendship is what makes the friendship stronger. Commitment is showing up in a time of need. It is not bailing at the last minute or making excuses after giving a word. True friends stay committed, and they always make sure that they will be there for us in times of trouble, and we can rely on them all the time.

We all know that 'Birds of a feather flock together.' A recent study has suggested that our choice of friends is dictated by shared interests more than our fondness for them. Friends with similar interests in sports, music, movies, books, and games can last longer in their friendship because it is more fun to be together if we share an interest. Such similar interests keep us glued together, helping us to understand each other better and also giving us a chance to learn something new in life.

Intimacy is built in a friendship when we share privileged information and disclose personal feelings. Feeling able to share some degree of personal information with any friend is necessary for a below-surface-level connection. An ability to be vulnerable is an indicator that we have a foundation of trust in place. To quote the Dalai Lama, "Genuine friendship can only be based on trust and affection, which can only arise when there is a mutual sense of concern and respect." We can't call someone a friend if we do not trust them. Trust and affection grow when there is mutual concern and respect. Having a trustworthy friend means being able to talk to them about a personal issue we are facing, knowing that what is said will stay between the 2 of us and that they will not judge you or the circumstance.

The one whom you trust and who becomes your confidante will be held in positive regard and gain all your affection. When you do like a friend, a spiral of positivity unfolds. Showing a friend that you like them makes them more likely to feel secure in the relationship. Love, trust, and affection for each other can deepen and strengthen the relationship, and eventually, it will become a true friendship.

There is one Zen story that describes true friendship. Once there were 2 friends. One plays the harp skilfully, and the other one listens to the music skilfully. When one plays a song about the mountains, the other would listen and say, "I can see the peaks in the distance." And when one plays a song about the ocean, the other would say, "I can see the waves before us." One day, the listener became ill and died. The first friend became sad, and he cut the strings of his harp and never played again. Since that time, the cutting of harp strings has always been a sign of intimate friendship.

A true friend always tries his best to cheer us up when we are sad or upset about something. Dr Jess Warner-Cohen, PhD, a clinical psychologist, says, "Often, as friends, we don't like to see people we care about in distress. But hard times happen to everyone. Recognising that sometimes someone just wants you to be with them and understanding the difficulty of the situation can really go a long way. It's not just telling someone that 'things will get better.' It's really showing up for them, letting them know you hear what they're saying and that you're truly here for them."

In her book *Frientimacy*, Shasta Nelson talks about the 3 requirements of all healthy friendships: positivity, consistency, and vulnerability. Friendship must bring joy and happiness, not exhaustion or stress. To be a good friend, one must be consistent in staying connected with friends. Only when we connect with friends can we discover new aspects of ourselves? Also, it is through vulnerability that we feel seen and known. We should not feel shy or ashamed to call a friend when in need and say, "I need to talk with you." Just being ourselves with our friends is a relief because a good friend will never judge us for how we truly are. One good friend is worth more than a thousand fake friends.

Nowadays, having many numbers of friends does not matter more than having a few good friends. Gone are the days when friends used to be counted on. Now, they are counted up. A multitude of friends makes socialising harder. Along with all the commitments in our hectic lives, we find it difficult to maintain our friendships. One scroll on social media feels like enough socialising for us, and we end up getting caught in the loneliness storm. So, how does one can be a good friend to someone and receive friendship in return?

"Don't wait for people to be friendly. Show them how," - unknown.

As the Swedish Proverb says, friendships double our joy and divide our grief. Good friends make us feel good. A good friend always listens and is genuinely interested in what we talk about. Even though there are differences, they handle the conflict respectfully. They allow us to be vulnerable and will be open-minded. They always ensure our safety and will never lead us into making poor decisions in our lives.

All individuals should attempt to cultivate good friendships that lead to the achievement of human flourishing and sustain the inherent meaning and values of life.

Chapter II
GOOD AND BAD FRIENDS

**A good friend is like a four-leaf clover:
hard to find and lucky to have.**

– Irish Proverb

In Greek legend, there were a pair of celebrated friends known for true friendship and sacrifice: Damon and Pythias. They lived in Syracuse, an important part of Sicily, and were very good friends who hardly ever saw each other apart. The 2 young men were called Damon and Pythias.

Pythias ran into trouble with a tyrant called Dionysius and ended up in prison. Dionysius condemned Pythias to die in a few days. When Damon heard of Pythias's punishment, he pleaded with the tyrant to release him, but in vain.

Pythias had an old mother and an unmarried sister back home. Before dying, he wanted to bid goodbye to them. When he spoke with his friend Damon, he said he would die peacefully if only he could take care of his mother and sister.

In order to gratify his friend's last wish, Damon went to the tyrant and proposed to take the place of Pythias in prison until he returned from home. He said he would even die for his friend if he did not return from his duty on time.

Dionysius, the tyrant, was surprised that anybody should make such an offer. He, at last, agreed to let Pythias go and gave orders that the young man Damon should be shut up in prison, with a warning that if Pythias were not back in time, Damon would have to die instead.

Pythias promised Damon that he would be back in a few days to release him. He rushed home, took care of his responsibilities, bid his mother farewell, and set out to return to Syracuse.

But on the way back to prison, he was caught up by thieves who tied him to a tree. After struggling for a long time, he managed to wrench himself free and sped along on his way. But then, on the way, he had to cross a torrent. With no second thought, he plunged into the water, fought the waves successfully and reached the shore. He sped fast, for he knew that his friend would die if he were not in Syracuse by sunset.

The last hour came. The guards led Damon to the place of crucifixion, where he sincerely hoped Pythias would come too late so that he might die in his stead. Just as the guards were about to nail Damon to the cross, Pythias entered. Running towards Damon, he hugged him and sobbed with relief. Damon, too, began to shed tears of bitter regret.

Pythias was happy because he thought that he had come in time, even though it was at the last moment. The tyrant, touched by seeing this true friendship, forgot his cruelty for once. He felt that men who loved and trusted each other this much should not suffer unjustly. So, he set them both free.

This friendship between Damon and Pythias has become proverbial. Their story has been a favourite with poets and playwrights, and men who were loyal and devoted friends were often compared with Damon and Pythias.

Friends who are loyal to each other go a long way in their friendship. Loyalty is the way to begin the building process of friendship. Loyal friends keep their promises and never disclose the private things shared between each other. Loyalty is being there for a friend in difficult times. The one quality that makes a good friend is presence. One does not have to go through difficult times to need a good friend. Sometimes, being present for a friend simply means listening to them when they talk. Lending your ears means so much in friendship. Listening to them and keeping focused on them will help them feel cared for.

Also, not being judgemental while listening also makes one a good friend. Good friends do not judge us for not hitting the gym as they do. They would not judge us for the clothes we wear, for speaking slang, or for caring way too much about something stupid. Friends accept the real us and love us for who we really are. We can expose our emotions and circumstances to each other and trust one another to listen, be supportive, and have each other's best interests at heart.

"Friendship is a single soul dwelling in 2 bodies," says the ancient Greek philosopher Aristotle. He wrote widely about what friends are and what makes good friends. He said good friends have sympathy and care for each other. He even identified 3 types of friendships:

- Friendship is based on utility.

- Friendship is based on pleasure.

- Friendship is based on the mutual appreciation of each other's values.

FRIENDSHIP BASED ON UTILITY:

Friendships of utility form when someone is useful to us in some way. In this kind of relationship, the 2 parties are not in it for the affection of one another but more so because each party receives a benefit in exchange. It's not permanent in nature, and whenever the benefit ends, so does the relationship that brought the parties together. Aristotle observed this to be more common in older folks.

A gym companion may become a friend, for they can be helpful to one another while lifting weights. A neighbour may become a friend, for she might take care of our plants when we are out of the station. This type of friendship is just a "hi-bye" relationship. Also, co-workers might have a utility friendship, even though they see each other almost daily and know a depth of information about each other. These co-workers know they must be cordial and professional within their environment, and both are working in a competitive field. Therefore, one of the co-workers may be using the relationship to learn as much as possible about their company and position. These people normally would not have such a strong connection outside of work but have formed a bond of necessity that has grown into a relationship.

FRIENDSHIP BASED ON PLEASURE:

Friendships of pleasure form between those who enjoy each other's company. This kind of friendship is more common in people who are younger. It's the kind of relationship frequently seen among college friends or people who participate in the same sports team. They are often called 'activity buddies.' Going for a long ride, partying together during weekends, or going together to the nail salon, buddies indulge in this type of friendship.

The source of such a friendship is more emotional, and it's often the most short-lived of the relationships. It's fine for as long as the 2 parties gain enjoyment through a mutual interest in something external, but it ends as soon as either tastes or preferences change.

Many young people go through different phases in their views on enjoyment, and quite often, the people in their lives tend to change as the phase they're in recalibrates over time.

FRIENDSHIP BASED ON MUTUAL APPRECIATION OF EACH OTHER'S VALUES:

The final form of friendship that Aristotle outlined is also the most preferable out of the 3. Rather than utility or pleasure, this kind of relationship is based on a mutual appreciation of the virtues that the other party holds dear.

Friendship of mutual appreciation takes a longer time to build because it is a powerful and more enduring friendship. It forms when 2 people accept each other's flaws and respect each other's values and goals. But when they do blossom, they do so with trust, admiration, and awe. They bring with them some of the sweeter joys that life has to offer.

Mostly, this type of friendship begins in childhood, adolescence, or during college days. The friendships based on utility or pleasure do not last long, whereas friendships based on virtues will stay strong. People who lack empathy or care for others seldom develop these kinds of relationships. There is, quite generally, a base level of goodness required in each person for it to exist in the first place.

Friends who stay together with respect and admiration for one another are called good friends. Good friends last until the end. They depend on mutual growth occurring. Beyond the depth and intimacy, the beauty of such relationships is that they automatically include the rewards of the other 2 kinds of friendship. They're pleasurable and beneficial.

When you respect a person and care for them, you gain joy from being with them. If they're a good enough person to warrant such a relationship to begin with, then there is utility too.

In today's context, these 3 kinds of friendships have taken on a new version: friends for a reason, friends for a season, and friends for a lifetime. A lifetime friendship requires interdependence and voluntary participation. "True friendships are hallmarked by each member's desire to engage with the other – it's about a mutual interest in one another's experiences and thoughts, as well as a sense of 'belongingness' and connection," says Northern Illinois University psychologist and friendship expert Dr Suzanne Degges-White.

According to Degges-White, there are 4 core types of friendship: acquaintance, friend, close friend, and best friend. Acquaintances are easy enough to categorise. They're the people who aren't complete strangers, whom you run into regularly at a place like the coffee shop or work cafeteria but you don't really know. "They are people we know well enough to make small talk with on a regular basis, but not really people we'd invite to a dinner party or call on if we needed assistance," she says.

Friends are those that we try to run into or mix with. They are the people whom we look for support and help. Close friends are the people with whom we trade our secrets. Degges-White elaborates: "There's not just a strong level of trust between these friends; there's also a lot of unconditional regard and affinity. You may not like a close friend's choices, but you'd defend her right to make them."

Last but not least is the truly few-and-far-between phenomenon of the "best friend." Best friends are the rarest type of friend and the kind of friend that we all need to have in our lives. It's the friend who gets you without you having to explain yourself. It's the type of friend who loves you no matter what. They're not necessarily people you talk to every day. "You might go weeks or months without connecting, but when you do reconnect, it's as if no time has passed at all. These friendships are different in their ability to flex and endure even if life temporarily gets in the way. These are 'heart-to-heart' or 'soul friends,' and they can give you comfort even if you're out of touch with this friend," says Degges-White.

Normally, people categorise friends as good friends and bad friends. They always use the word 'good' to indicate someone who is a close friend. But the word 'good' indicates the goodness of a person who can be our quality friend. Certain characteristics and qualities of a person make a friend 'good.'

CHARACTERISTICS OF A GOOD FRIEND:

Anyone you call a friend should live up to certain standards. Knowing the characteristics of a good friend can help you appreciate your current friendships and make new, meaningful connections.

1. Good friends live with integrity. They have strong moral principles, values, and commitments. They speak and behave in a consistent manner.

2. Good friends are trustworthy. Not only are your secrets safe with them, but so are your vulnerability, fear, and weirdness.

3. Good friends are dependable. They show up and keep their promises.

4. They're loyal. Friends who have integrity are loyal to the people they care about and who have been with them through ups and downs. They don't speak negatively about you; they listen to your side of the story, give you the benefit of the doubt, and defend you when you deserve it.

5. Good friends have empathy for others. They put themselves in your shoes, understand what you're feeling, and react accordingly.

6. They're good listeners. They give room for us to speak and ask questions, so that we can validate our emotions and find a perspective.

7. Their confidence is contagious. A good friend is comfortable with themselves and with whomever they are friends with. Real confidence is an important trait for any friend. It will inspire us and make us feel confident, too.

8. Spending time with them makes you feel good.

9. Good friends are fun to be with. A sense of humour is always helpful. Good friends know how to hit your funny bone and appreciate your quirks.

10. They're non-judgemental. Good friends never make you feel bad for being yourself. They accept you for who you are, with all the flaws and imperfections.

11. A good friend is someone who is honest and never lies to a friend. Honesty plays an important role in any relationship. It is the foundation of trust in friendships, too. Trust and honesty work in harmony, as do love and honesty.

We are often friends with people because they are similar to us. However, the most successful relationships are those where both parties have complementary attributes. A bad friend is hard to spot and hard to figure out. It takes time and patience to realise that there is a problem with your friendship.

Here are some characteristics of a bad friend:

1. Bad friends are disrespectful: they speak about you and talk behind your back.

2. They always want to take from you. They seldom give when they have but demand a lot from us. Not only material possessions but also the time and effort we put into our friendship.

3. They have unrealistic expectations. They may be setting unrealistic expectations for you or asking for favours that are too much for you to handle.

4. They consider you as their last option. Be it going out for a party or getting a career-oriented opportunity, you come to their mind only at the last minute or never.

5. They are unsupportive: They don't really care about how you feel or if you need emotional support.

6. They become unhappy when something good happens to them. They will only pretend to celebrate our success, but truly, they feel envious of our achievements.

The consequences of having such bad friends might not seem like they matter at first, but it's important that we consider what could happen if we keep those kinds of relationships going on for too long. Such friendships become toxic, and they will bring negative impacts. Bad friendships affect our self-esteem and happiness. A toxic friendship can cause a lot of damage—emotional, mental, and even physical damage. Not all toxic friendships are easy to leave. But being aware of the signs will make it easier for you to have the power you have to limit the bad friendship.

Chapter III

TYPES OF FRIENDS

"Friendship is the only cement that will ever hold the world together,"

– Woodrow T. Wilson

Sometimes, we meet someone new, and in an instant, we know we are going to be close friends. Other times, it takes longer to get to know someone until we feel comfortable enough to put our walls down. But once we find our tribe, life becomes fun and exciting. Different types of friends make our life feel fuller. Though we feel content with our one good friend, we feel happiest when we are in large, diverse groups. We all need a diverse, well-rounded entourage that will stick with us through thick and thin. Here are the 4 types of friends who would keep our life more meaningful and happier.

1. **Life-long Friends:**

   Life-long friends are friends of many years. Life-long friends know they can count on each other to be there through it all with a listening ear, a shoulder to cry on, or just a welcome distraction in a heartbreak. They will always remember our birthdays and anniversaries. They know what our favourite dessert and favourite colour are. They always remember to check in on things we have mentioned, be it a hospital appointment or a job interview; they remember what we were nervous about.

19

A life-long friend can see you at your very worst and still love you unconditionally. No matter how much you may vent, how much you may cry, or how much you may express anger, this friend will remember who you are at the very core, and you need not worry about them loving you any less at those times when you feel your worst.

Life-long friends are good friends and close friends. They can also be called 2 am friends. A friend who will come to our aid at a moment's notice is called a 2 am friend. The urban dictionary defines a 2 am friend as somebody you can message or talk to late at night. 2 am is said to be an unearthly hour because no human being will be reachable at such an odd hour. However, good friends are always reachable and approachable, no matter what time it is. They will be willing to drop everything and come support you at those times when you need them most. If you call a life-long friend shortly after a breakup, or if you're left to deal with the aftermath of a major car accident, your friend is willing to cancel plans just to be with you when you need them.

Everyone must have a 2 am friend in their lives. When life throws us a curveball, it is essential to have a 2 am friend who would be upset if we don't reach them in the time of our need. 2 am friends are selfless. Even if we have not spoken to them in a long, long time, they will fly around the world to help us with our needs. There will always be real closeness and an unbreakable trust. Such friends are not easy to find, though. Only a few can be really considered as 2 am friends, and if we have one, we should not even think of letting them go.

Such good friends bask in each other's joys, feeling true happiness for one another when something positive happens in life. There is no jealousy, no envy, and no selfishness here. A good friend might think of ways to celebrate your big promotion or new home with you or might ask you to give them a detailed account of something wonderful that happened to you, truly feeling, with you, the same happiness that you are feeling.

Life-long friends are not afraid to talk about difficult things. They will be honest with us and even share something when there is a rift in the friendship. They might even tell you something difficult that you truly need to hear in a loving way when others might shy away from communicating it.

Every set of life-long friends has its own way of battling through hardships together. But generally, good friends will empathise together by actively listening, offering non-intrusive expressions of sympathy, and offering a hug or pat on the back when needed. Life-long friends don't merely support one another when needed; they know how to support one another.

Similarly, life-long friends simply trust one another. They trust each other with their deepest feelings and secrets. They trust one another to watch children, hold spare house keys, and be emergency contacts. They know that they will never betray one another. With life-long friends, trust simply isn't a question.

Good friends don't have to have everything in common, but they will have something significant in common. Maybe they share similar spiritual beliefs, or maybe they have the same sense of humour. It could be a shared passion as well, such as a love for running or reading. While some friendships might be built on something fleeting, like shared substance abuse, the most lasting of friendships are built on something much more substantial.

Friends who enjoy a strong, lasting friendship will remain friends, no matter where their respective paths take them. Even if they end up miles apart, and even if months or years pass between meeting with one another, it will be as if no time at all has passed when they reunite. We can always count on our long-time friends to show up when we really need them.

Life-long friends are our best friends because they will make us feel like our best selves around them. The deepest friendships make us feel completely comfortable around our friends.

2. **BFF:**

BFF is a short form for Best Friends Forever. Best friends are like security blankets. A moment spent with them will give us a comforted and secure feel and take away all the anxiety from us. In fact, those who give us such a feeling can only be termed BFFs.

Not all friends can become BFFs. Though friends bring happiness and joy to us, only a best friend can be considered the personification of the ultimate friendship. The level of casualness is not the same among a group of friends. Some friends consider themselves still strangers because of the lack of intimacy. Best friends are more acquainted and intimate not only with us but also with our family members and other friends. The deeper level of intimacy is what makes them be called "Best Friend Forever."

A best friend is someone who knows all about us. To our best friends, we can share all our secrets without hiding anything and be just what we are. With them, our secrets will remain secretive, and we know for sure that they will never disclose our secrets in any circumstance. They will forever be our confidant, and if needed, they will come to our rescue in troubles. This is what makes us feel secure and comforted.

3. **Social Group Friends:**

Social group friends are those who come together in a social circle. They can be our neighbours or friends at a club. Social group friends share a common interest, and that common interest brings people together. Friends in a social circle may share a deeper level of interaction and communication. People in our social circle know more about our personal lives, and we manage to catch-up with each other once in a while and talk as if time has not passed by, even after months of being away from each other. We can tell the difference between an acquaintance and a social friend because social friends are so happy when we are happy, even if they are not completely fond of or completely agree with all of our decisions in your life.

A social friend is someone who may ask for favours but will also complete favours for us in return. They may need something or talk to us about a problem they are facing, but in return, they ask us about our problems and try to assist us.

Social friends are complimentary friends, cannot keep secrets from others. They may gossip around about us, but social friends are essential in our life because they are totally reliable in times of trouble. They will be the ones who would first lend their helping hand for us, but they are not like our best friends who help us and expect from us nothing in return.

4. **Activity Friends:**

Activity friends are fun friends. They are probably more of an acquaintance. They're someone who you see at parties and who loves to invite you to various events. They've always got something going on, and when you're together, it's all about the fun.

Sometimes, activity friends can also be termed as fair-weather friends because they will be there with us when things are going well in our lives. But they disappear during our rough patches. Fair-weather friends are only committed during fun times. They will be there when everything is going smoothly, but once we disagree on something, they will see us as their enemy. Sometimes, we also choose to be with friends who agree with and accept our views and opinions. We gravitate towards those who support us. It is natural to seek friends with mutual admiration. Such fair-weather friendships are shallow, even though they feel like good relationships. Let me explain why.

- Fair-weather friends never are with us in our problems. They always think any difficulty we face is our problem, and they let us handle it by ourselves without giving us any support.

- They always want us to accept them as they are. Justifying or trying to get an explanation for their unreceptivity is not appreciated by them. Processing the differences in their friendship is considered fruitless.

- They embrace the principle of "believing in yourself." If, at all, we try to reach them in our hard times, all we get from them is, "Why do you need me? Just believe in yourself. You will be fine."

- Fair-weather friends do not accept criticisms. If we accuse them of not being there for us in our troubles, they will play the victim, saying, "You are a drama queen; stop being rude to me; you don't know what I am going through, and you always think only of yourself." An instant table-turning will happen in their defence, and we find ourselves ending up apologising for bringing up the conversation at all.

- They are quick to diagnose us for being emotional when we challenge them.

- They always take us for granted. One way or another, they make us feel unheard.

- Fair-weather friends want us to trust them and hold on to them, even when they make us feel abandoned.

A fair-weather friend is someone who's there for the good stuff. They want to hear about the cute thing your cat did or the promotion you just got, but they're not someone you confide in when it comes to the heavy stuff. A fair-weather friend is basically a surface-level friend. It's not necessarily a bad thing, as long as you're realistic about what the friendship is. If you've tried confiding in them about more emotional stuff and they're always a bit standoffish, but they don't hesitate to come to you with their own emotional stuff, then you may want to re-evaluate things. There's nothing wrong with surface-level relationships as long as they're even. Don't give more than you're getting back.

Having fair-weather friends is okay, but we must also have a thorough understanding that we can't count on them. Also, we must be sure not to act like a fair-weather friend, particularly when our friends need us. Sometimes, the fun friend can become toxic if the partying goes to an unhealthy place. Have fun with the fun friend when the situation warrants it, but we must remember that life is all about balance.

We all have read the story of 2 friends and a bear. Once, 2 friends were passing through a forest. Out of nowhere came a bear and began to grunt. The 2 friends got terrified and tried to get away from the place as soon as possible. One friend ran hard and climbed up a tree. The other, who does not know how to climb a tree, got scared and laid himself on the ground. He lay there pretending to be dead. The bear came near him. It looked down on him and sniffed him. He felt so scared, and he held his breath even. The bear, after sniffing him hard, took him for dead and went away.

Now, the fair-weather friend who managed to escape himself by climbing up the tree came down. He asked the other friend, "What did the bear whisper into your ears?" He answered that the bear had advised him to beware of fair-weather friends.

A true friend foregoes his own pleasure and convenience for the sake of his friend. Friends are chosen, family. They lift our heads and hearts, like how a family member would do. In the Holy Bible, a verse goes like this: "A friend loveth at all times, and a brother is born for adversity" (Proverbs 17:17). Despite intensifying hardships, a friend is there to comfort and help, unlike a fair-weather friend.

In the book of Job in the Bible, there is a lesson on friendship.

The job was a righteous man. He had a wife, sons, daughters, servants, and large herds of livestock. He was righteous and faithful to God. When Satan pointed out to God that only because of his riches he is being faithful, God decided to allow Satan to test Job in order to prove to Satan that a righteous man would still be faithful in all circumstances. During the test, Job lost all his riches. He even lost his sons and daughters, and only his wife was left behind. Job also felt sick with boils and sores all over his body. He was about as low as a man can get on this Earth. But in all this, Job did not sin or speak against God.

His 3 close friends, Eliphaz, Bildad, and Zophar, heard of his affliction, and they came to see him. They sat with him for 7 days and nights and said nothing, just mourned with him. After 7 days of mourning, they started to speak to him. They began a long, miserable debate about the reasons for Job's suffering. They told Job that it was his fault that he was suffering. Job was confused and frustrated because he knew God was just, but he also knew that he had done no sin. When his friends kept attacking him and insisted that his suffering was his own doing, Job called out to God for proof. Eventually, God rebuked the friends and blessed Job even more than before.

In the *Book of Job*, it is mentioned more than once that Job was a righteous man, but his friends apparently did not know and understand Job and his righteousness. If they had spent the time to really get to know him, they would have believed and trusted Job. They would have spoken words of comfort to him.

Fair-weather friends fail to listen to each other or to provide comfort and support. There are times when all we need is a prayer, an encouraging word, a shoulder to lean on, cry with, or a comforting hug. Sometimes, when we are lonely, we become so desperate for human connections and end up connected to fair-weather friends. We might think, "Okay! Now we have a good many friends to look after us. So, the next time we feel lonely, they will be there for us, just a text message away." But with fair-weather friends, things do not work that way. We send text messages and messages in a row only to receive nothing back from them. All our messages can go without response.

Fair-weather friends can cancel plans to meet up without any second thought. Ghosting friends comes effortlessly to them. Success and egos can tear such friendships apart. Friendship breaks happen when we are friends with fair-weather friends. Building quality friendships is essential in this 21ˢᵗ century. Quality friendships cannot happen without investing some effort, time, dedication, honesty, and vulnerability on both sides. When one cannot find these qualities in a fair-weather friend, accepting them as they are is the best way to retain our friendship. Just because we are not as close to them as we used to be, we cannot value our friendship less. Accept that this is a fair-weather friend, and that is all it will ever be.

If the friendship becomes toxic and it is taking all our peace, it is okay to let it go. Because everyone deserves to be loved for who we are. We deserve respect for what we stand for and to be told that on a regular basis. If it is not happening in a friendship, letting go of it is the only option left.

Chapter IV

THE ICONIC FRIENDSHIPS IN INDIAN MYTHOLOGY

In the sweetness of friendship, let there be laughter and sharing of pleasures. For in the dew of little things, the heart finds its morning and is refreshed

– Khalil Gibran

We bind with people through blood ties. Our parents, relatives, siblings, and cousins are part of our lives without our choice. It is nature's way of binding us with people. But our friends are whom we choose. We choose to include them to be a part of our life, so we must choose them wisely. Once we have made the choice of our friends, the love and joy we share with them is immense.

In India, people celebrate friendships like they celebrate any other human relationships. True friendships are celebrated in every aspect of our culture. There are numerous virtues of friendship in the treasure trove of Indian legends. Here are a few anecdotes from Indian Mythology which depict the essence of friendship.

1. **The Friendship Between Krishna and Sudama:**

   The story of Krishna and Sudama's friendship is one such inspiring friendship story in which Krishna helped Sudama in his adversity.

Krishna and Sudama were childhood friends. They studied together in the Gurukul.

Eventually, Krishna became a king. But his friend Sudama was a poor man. He had no money or assets, and he and his wife were struggling to make ends meet.

One day, Sudama's wife asked him to go to Krishna to ask for some help. Feeling shy, Sudama said, "How can I ask a friend for something? I don't feel like doing it."

But finding no other way to make a living, he decides to meet Krishna. He packed some rice crispies for Krishna since he couldn't go empty-handed when meeting a friend. So, he packed the rice crispies in a piece of cloth and took them to Krishna.

He entered Krishna's beautifully decorated palace. Krishna was sitting on his throne, and there were so many servants around him. The moment he saw Sudama, he rushed to him and treated him with the utmost kindness. He washed Sudama's feet and made him sit on his throne. Then he asked Sudama, "What have you brought for me? Come on, give me!"

Krishna is always mischievous, and he knows that Sudama is feeling shy. So, to tease him, he asked, "What have you brought?"

Looking at the grandeur of the palace and Krishna's kindness, Sudama felt even more shy and thought, "How can I offer these rice crispies?" But then Krishna grabbed hold of them and started to stuff his mouth with the rice crispies. Sudama felt happy at this gesture and completely forgot why he had come to meet his friend. Krishna forgot to give him anything or ask about the purpose of his visit.

When 2 souls meet in such a deep friendship, they forget everything.

After some time, Sudama thanked Krishna and left the palace. However, when he went back to his home, he found his whole house had been transformed. He now had all the riches in his house. His wife was very happy. Without asking and without giving, Sudama's adversity was changed.

2. **Karna and Duryodhana's Friendship:**

Karna and Duryodhana are the 2 individuals who are significantly different in social standing.

Duryodhana was a Kaurava prince. He was a man of great valour, loved and admired by all the people. At the same time, Karna was not born to royal parents. He was the son of Kunti, the mother of the Pandavas, and Surya, the Sun God. He was the half-brother of the Pandavas. His mother, Kunti, abandoned him as a child, so he was raised by a charioteer. All his life, he did not know that he was born a prince but believed that he was born to a charioteer. He respected his loving parents but always felt bad that he could not be a prince.

Karna and Duryodhana's friendship began during a competition. The competition was held in Hastinapur. Everyone was invited to come forward and show their skills and strength. The Pandavas showed their javelin-throwing skills and fighting skills. People were cheering, and they were waiting for Arjuna to show his skill in archery. At the same time, Arjuna was performing his skills in archery, and a feeling of competency awoke in Karna. He thought if given a chance, he could easily match and even up with Arjuna's skills. So, he challenged Arjuna, who also accepted. But Drona thought if Karna won the challenge, Arjuna might lose his reputation among the people. He asked Karna about his parents and to which kingdom he belonged.

Karna hung his head in shame because he knew only the royal princes could participate in those games. He felt defeated.

Duryodhana, who was shocked by Drona's attitude, walked up to Karna and embraced him. "Where are you from, my friend?" asked Duryodhana. Karna could not reply. Realising the cause of

Karna's silence, Duryodhana announced him as the King of Anga, a small province that was under the rule and care of Duryodhana. He also claimed that Karna was no ordinary person and his best friend, which is why he should be allowed to participate in the competition.

Karna was touched by the love and nobility of Duryodhana. He felt moved by Duryodhana's affection in giving him a province even without knowing anything about him. He asked Duryodhana what he wanted in return, to which Duryodhana replied that he just wanted Karna to be his loyal and faithful friend.

Thus began a friendship that defied all odds and gave Karna a much-deserved chance to fight a war, showing his worth and skills in the war of Kurukshetra.

3. **Lord Krishna and Arjuna's Friendship:**

The friendship between Lord Krishna and Arjuna is eternal. They had selfless love and affection for one another.

Their friendship began during the event of Draupadi Swayamvar, where Krishna finds out that Arjuna is in the disguise of a Brahmin. A battle began between Arjuna, Karna, Bhima, and Shalya. Krishna intervened and stopped the battle. After this, Krishna participated actively in various events in the life of the Pandavas, and that's how the bond between Krishna and Arjuna was cemented. Thereafter, they grew fond of each other and were together almost all the time.

Once, a Brahmin came to Lord Krishna and accused him of being an incapable ruler. He said that Lord Krishna was unable to protect his children, and his children died. Arjuna, who was with Krishna at that moment, felt very bad, and they both went to the Brahmin's home. Arjuna promised the Brahmin that he would protect the children. The Brahmin asked, "How will you protect my children?" Arjuna replied that he had the bow of Ghandiva, the strongest in the world, and he would be able to defeat anyone.

Arjuna made a shield of arrows for the entire house. Krishna was watching all this silently. The Brahmin's wife got pregnant once again, but this time, as soon as the child was born, it disappeared into thin air. The Brahmin was furious and accused Arjuna of not keeping his word.

Arjuna, feeling dejected, decided to give up his life. Krishna consoled Arjuna and took him in his chariot. Arjuna had no clue as to where Krishna was taking him. They entered into a dark cave. Krishna ordered his Sudarshana to light the way. At the end of the cave, they found the most amazing scene ever. Arjuna saw Lord Vishnu sitting on the serpent Ananta Shesha with all the children playing around him. Lord Vishnu explained to Arjuna that all these incidents were intended to teach Arjuna a lesson of humility. Arjuna apologised to Lord Vishnu, and he and Lord Krishna brought all the children back safely to the Brahmin.

Many such instances portray the ideal bond that existed between Lord Krishna and Arjuna. Sanjaya testified to this great and unique friendship with Dhritarashtra when he came back after visiting the Pandavas. He said that the friendship between Lord Krishna and Arjuna was so strong that there was no secret or privacy between them.

Once, when Lord Krishna went to the forest to meet the Pandavas, he told Arjuna, *"You are mine; similarly, I am yours. My friends are your friends. Whoever shows enmity to you is my enemy too; whoever stands by you also stands by me."*

Such love Krishna had for Arjuna. It is said that when Krishna first met Arjuna, he embraced Arjuna wholeheartedly, and tears came to his eyes because Arjuna reminded Krishna of His intimate cowherd friend in Vraja of the same name. Krishna and Arjuna became instant companions and spent many years together in deep friendship.

In the Mahabharata (Sauptika Parva, XII), Krishna states, *"I have no dearer friend on Earth than Arjuna, and there is nothing that I cannot give to him, including my wives and children."*

In the Drona Parva of the same text, Krishna reiterates, *"O Daruka, I shall not be able to cast my eyes, even for a single moment, on the Earth bereft of Arjuna… Know that Arjuna is half of my body."*

4. **Trijata–Sita Friendship:**

Trijata was a demoness in the service of Ravana. Ravana abducted Sita and brought her to his palace. When Sita refused to stay in the palace of Ravana, she was sent to Ashoka Vatika. Ravana appointed demonesses to guard and take care of Sita. He instructed them to convince Sita to forget Rama and marry him.

All the demonesses took Ravana's orders very seriously and started harassing a distraught Sita. They were exceptionally rude to her and treated her with disrespect. They spoke to her about the greatness of their king, Ravana, and said that she should consider herself lucky that their king wanted to marry her.

Sita was already feeling dejected, for she was abducted by Ravana and brought to a land far away from her husband. The taunts and rude behaviour of the demonesses made her feel even more depressed and lonely. The only relief came to Sita in the form of Trijata.

Trijata stepped in when the other demonesses were harassing her and narrated to them about her prophetic dream. It was about Lanka getting burnt down by a vanara (monkey), and Lord Rama coming to rescue Sita. Trijata asks the demonesses to apologise to Sita, and since Trijata is the oldest one, they obeyed her.

Trijata's words comforted Sita. She felt relieved in the presence of Trijata. Trijata became the only silver lining for Sita during the period of her captivity.

Over time, Trijata became Sita's confidante. Trijata was the only warm relationship she developed in her captivity.

When Lord Rama came with his vanara sena to rescue her, Ravana asked Trijata to accompany Sita to the battlefield. There is a point where Sita thinks Rama has died and became distraught with grief. Trijata was the one who reassured her that Lord Rama is very much alive and would come to rescue her from the clutches of the evil king.

Trijata realised the chaste power of Sita when she had the dream where Ravan, Indrajeet, and Kumbhakarn fell to their doom. She dreamt of Lord Rama and Lakshmana riding the Airavat with Sita seated in his lap. She also saw the 3 of them flying towards Ayodhya in Pushpak Viman. Additionally, she saw in her dream that Ravan, Indrajeet, and Kumbhakran were drenched in oil and heading south on a donkey. She saw the pious Vibhishan in white garments riding a royal elephant. Her prophetic dream ended with the vision of Lanka getting submerged in the ocean.

When she narrated her dream to Sita, it soothed her, and she hoped that she would be united with Lord Rama soon. Trijata's dream came true exactly as she dreamt. Sita was rescued by her husband, Lord Rama, exactly as Trijata explained to her.

Trijata proved to be one of the selfless traits of a woman who put all her intellect into giving confidence and comfort to Mata Sita. She proved that dharma can be practised even though born in a demon clan. She was the most loyal, trustworthy, and confidential companion to Sita and gave her all the love of a mother. Sita listened to each and every event recounted by Trijata of Lord Rama's march on Lanka with great hope and happiness. Trijata's unconditional service to Sita became the greatest relief to her in her difficult times. Trijata was the true friend of Sita.

5. **Friendship Between Lord Krishna and Draupadi:**

Lord Krishna and Draupadi's friendship in the Mahabharata was one such friendship. They were best friends and loved each other as friends. Krishna called her 'Sakhi,' and she called him 'Sakha.'

Sakha means friend. The 'SAKHYA' or friendship shared between them was of deep understanding of each other's commitments, joys, and travails of life. They were always there for each other. The love they had for each other was pure friendship.

Once, Krishna cut his little finger while handling sugarcane. His queen, Sathyabama, immediately sent for help. His other consort, Rukmini, rushed to bring some clothes herself. Draupadi, who was nearby, tore off a part of her saree and bandaged Krishna's bleeding finger. Touched by this selfless token of affection, Krishna promised to protect her in times of distress. He uttered the word 'Akshayam,' which means 'unending.' Their friendship proved to be an unending one.

As promised, Lord Krishna saved Draupadi from shame. During the infamous dice game with Duryodhan and his uncle Shakuni, Yudhishthir lost all his wealth, kingdom, and his 4 brothers – Bheem, Arjun, Nakul, and Sahadeva. When he lost everything and had nothing to play with, he put his and his brothers' common wife, Draupadi, into the gamble. He lost her too in the game. So, the evil Duryodhan asked his equally evil brother, Dushashan, to drag Draupadi into court and strip her in front of others. Dushasan succeeded in dragging her to the court. This is when Draupadi started praying to Krishna to save her. Krishna, through his powers, ensured that the length of her garment didn't end, and Dushasan did not succeed in stripping her. Finally, an exhausted Dushashan gave up, and Draupadi was saved. After she was saved, she cried bitter tears and cried to Krishna, "Though you saved me at the last moment, you were not there, and this is what they did to me. Until I see Dushasana's blood, I cannot forget this." Krishna took a vow then. He said, "The heavens may fail. The Himalayas may be levelled. The seas may run dry as a dead man's bones. The Earth herself may burst asunder, but I will keep my oath to you. To avenge the crime against you, there will be a war to end all wars. Your eyes, which shed drops of fire today, will see all one hundred Kauravas dead upon the battlefield. Wipe your tears because the tears are the prerogative of the one hundred widows in Hastinapur." Such was the friendship between Draupadi and Krishna.

The foundation of the friendship between Lord Krishna and Draupadi is their mutual faith and respect. They had a deep understanding of each other and respected one another equally. The respect they had resulted in faith towards each other, and through many circumstances in their life, they showed a great amount of mutual understanding and faith. The common characteristic between them is their ability to read the other person with all of their emotions and to judge on all possible parameters.

Like good attracts good, Draupadi and Krishna formed a magnetic relationship. Their friendship was founded on pure love and is the epitome of the emotional aspect of self-exploration. She had a strong faith in the power of thoughts. Throughout her life, Draupadi tried to attain "oneness" with Krishna's thoughts because she believed these would help her surpass all hindrances and achieve her goal. This connection brings completeness to Draupadi's character and makes her life a beautiful and complete picture.

They loved and cared for each other. The love and care resulted in Krishna's divine intervention at the time of the disrobing of Draupadi in the royal assembly hall. Their friendship made their lives more meaningful and accomplished. Not only Draupadi but Krishna also honoured her. Therefore, at the time of disrobing, she called for his help. Krishna also encouraged Draupadi to live a life without the pressures of society. As a result, she followed her instinct and achieved the best in her life. Krishna and Draupadi were the best friends of Indian Mythology.

Chapter V

FRIENDSHIP IN BUDDHISM AND JAINISM

FRIENDSHIP IN BUDDHISM:

Friendship is a kind of virtue necessary for life. A good friend is a virtuous friend. In Buddhism, a virtuous friend is called *Kalyana Mitta*. A friend who is par excellence is known as *Kalyana Mitta*. The Buddha said that friendship is the whole of holy life. To accomplish it, we need only overcome our fear of reaching out to one another. When the Buddha's cousin Ananda approached him and remarked, *"This is half of the holy life, Lord: admirable friendship, admirable companionship, admirable camaraderie,"* the Buddha replied, *"Don't say that, Ananda. Don't say that. Admirable friendship, admirable companionship, and admirable camaraderie are actually the whole of the holy life. When a monk has admirable people as friends, companions, and comrades, he can be expected to develop and pursue the noble eightfold path."*

The Buddha explains what admirable friendship is. Friendship that teaches virtues and generosity and convicts one to be a good human being is true friendship. To quote his words, *"And what is meant by admirable friendship? There is the case where a layperson, in whatever town or village he may dwell, spends time with householders or householders' sons, young or old, who are advanced in virtue. He talks with them and engages them in discussions. He emulates consummate conviction in those who are consummate in conviction, consummate virtue in those who are consummate in virtue, consummate generosity in those who are consummate in*

37

generosity, and consummate discernment in those who are consummate in discernment. This is called admirable friendship."

According to Buddhism, a true spiritual friend is the enlightened one who can guide us on the path of liberation. A man's entire life is established on good friends. People often mistake the teachings of Buddha for non-attachment. They interpret his teachings that one should not associate with friends or others. They think one should renounce love and friendship. What Buddhism actually insists on is to guard against the passions that characterise jealousy, anger, lust, pride, or other bonds. The Buddha warned only against the dangers of over-attachment and possessiveness, and he spoke highly of true friendship and its positive qualities.

He even addresses many bhikkhus (male monastics), bhikkhunis (female monastics), upasakas (male laypeople), and upasikas (female laypeople) as "friends" when talking with them.

The Buddha distinguishes between true friends and false friends. In the *Kalyana Mitta Sutta*, he says, *"My Teaching is well proclaimed, and it is the intimate friendship with good friends and good associates, not the intimate friendship with evil friends and evil associates"* (SN 3.18).

True friends are trustworthy, worthy of friendship, and reliable throughout life, unlike false friends. In the Hiri Sutta, the Buddha comments on the qualities of false friends and true friends, saying that *"he on whom one can rely, like a child sleeping on its mother's breast, is truly a friend who cannot be parted from one by others"* (SN 2.3).

The Buddha also says, *"It is in dependence on me as an admirable friend that beings subject to birth have gained release from birth, that beings subject to ageing have gained release from ageing, that beings subject to death have gained release from death, that beings subject to sorrow, lamentation, pain, distress, & despair have gained release from sorrow, lamentation, pain, distress, & despair."*

The Buddha gives advice about associating with good friends. A good friend is someone who does not take advantage of the friendship. There will be no insincerity, flattery, or any harm in a true friendship. The Buddha says a good friend is always helpful, unconditional, sympathetic, and unwavering in his friendship. He asks his disciples to gather inspiration from such good friends. He talks about the 4 qualities that lead to a person's happiness and well-being. They are Being consummate in initiative, being consummate in vigilance, admirable friendship, and maintaining one's livelihood in tune.

An admirable friend is a warm-hearted friend who is a helpmate, who is the same in happiness and sorrow, who gives good counsel, and who sympathises.

A Buddhist monk who has an admirable friend will abandon what is unskillful and develop what is skilful. Friendship with good people is considered the prerequisite for self-awakening. In the Sambodhi Sutta, the Buddha says, "If wanderers who are members of other sects should ask you, 'What, friend, are the prerequisites for the development of the wings to self-awakening?' you should answer, 'There is the case where a monk has admirable friends, admirable companions, admirable comrades.' This is the first prerequisite for the development of the wings to self-awakening."

According to Buddhism, there are 4 types of friends we should meet and seek. They are:

1.   The helper,

2.   The enduring friend,

3.   The mentor and,

4.   The compassionate friend.

1.   **The Helper:**

The friend who comes under the category of the helper can be identified by 4 things:

- He will protect you when you are vulnerable.

- He will act as a refuge when you are afraid.

- When he requests something, he will provide double.

- He will always be there in thick and thin without expecting anything in return.

Such friends also protect your wealth and stop you from losing money. They give you the best guidance and show you the right path when you are lost or acting carelessly. The helper friend is always a giver, not a taker.

2. **The enduring friend:**

The enduring friend can be identified by 4 things:

- They tell their secrets to you.

- They guard our secrets like their own.

- They will not abandon us in our misfortune.

- They will even die for you.

The enduring friend is a non-judgemental person. They accept you for who you really are. They trust you and share all their secrets with you. Also, they will guard your secrets till the last. Unlike a toxic friend who will take advantage of your weaknesses and conspire against you, the enduring friend maintains confidentiality and stays true to their friendship.

An enduring friend never abandons you, even if you have hit rock bottom in your life, and is even ready to die for you. One can always count on an enduring friend. When making new friends, one must always check how they treat other people who are lower or higher in status than them. How they treat the lowest people is an indication of how they would treat you when you, too, are in the same position.

3. **The mentor:**

The mentor friends can be identified by the following characteristics:

- They guide you towards good deeds.

- They restrain you from your wrongdoings.

- They tell you what you ought to know,

- They show you the path to the heavens.

Like a good teacher or parent, the mentor friend will teach you through love, kindness, their own actions, and compassion. They will always speak the truth and share information backed up by scientific evidence.

The mentor friends deal with you patiently. They truly want to set an example. They are straightforward people who can help you get a complete picture of the circumstances by sharing their knowledge and experiences. One can always rely on mentor friends while making life's important decisions. By taking their wise advice, you can avoid wasting time, making mistakes, and learning lessons.

The mentor friends are good examples of trustworthiness and integrity.

4. **The compassionate friend:**

Compassionate friends can be identified by 4 things:

- They will not rejoice in your misfortune.

- They delight in your good fortune.

- They prevent others from speaking ill of you.

- They encourage those who praise your good qualities highly.

The compassionate friend is someone who showers you with love and happiness. They express their love and kindness through words and actions. They praise your high qualities.

These are the 4 types of friends we should seek and cherish according to Buddha. The Buddha advises us to let go of the persons who do not have these qualities of a helper, compassionate, enduring, and mentor friend.

The Buddha also warns us to beware of 4 enemies who come in disguise as friends. He advised the son of a homeowner, Sigala, about the 4 enemies. The 4 enemies are:

1.   The taker.

2.   The talker.

3.   The flatterer.

4.   The reckless companion.

The Buddha summed it up in a verse, saying, *"The friend who is all talk, and the friend who is empty of words, and the friend who is full of compliments, and the reckless friend. These 4 are not friends but enemies. The wise understand this and keep them at a distance, as they are a path beset by danger."*

1.   **The Taker:**

The takers are identified by 4 things:

- They only take. They do not give.
- They always ask for a lot but hardly give anything back.
- They perform their duties out of fear.
- They always offer services only to gain something.

2.   **The Talker:**

The talkers are identified by 4 things:

- They always remind us of past generosity.
- They promise future generosity.
- They speak with a flattering disposition.
- They protest personal misfortune when called on to help.

3.   **The Flatterer:**

The flatterers are identified by 4 things:

- They support good behaviour.
- They indiscriminately support bad behaviour, too.
- They praise you to your face

- They put you down behind your back.

4. **The Reckless Companion:**

The reckless companions are identified by 4 things:

- They are accompanied by drinking.

- They like to roam around at night.

- They like to party all the time.

- They gamble.

Thus, the Buddha explained well and broke down friends who are enemies in disguise. It is important to reflect on these points. We all know about the reckless companion. The overuse of alcohol and partying is a problem. A reckless companion will lead to more troubles in our lives. The Buddha always warned about the consumption of substances and a lifestyle that creates negative or unwholesome situations or thoughts. It is also important to note the flatterer who has an inability to point out bad behaviour. This would allow us to miss opportunities to better ourselves. A friend like a flatterer will not help us grow stronger in our lives.

The Buddha informs us that the spiritual path is "good friendship, good companionship, good comradeship." His teachings found in kalyā□amitta are about wise and empathetic friendships. If we are to develop the tools lauded in the dharma, which are empathy, compassion, calm reflection, and embodied awareness, we need to undo the impulses compelling us to fight, flee, shut down, or fall into spirals of self-loathing. Good friendship will enlighten us and help us to move forward on the spiritual path.

FRIENDSHIP IN JAINISM:

Jainism is one of the 3 most ancient religions of India. Its roots go back to the mid-first century B.C.E. Jainism is still an integral part of our Indian culture. Jainism teaches that the path to enlightenment is through nonviolence and reducing harm to living things (including plants and animals) as much as possible.

Jains believe bad karma is caused by harming living things. To avoid bad karma, Jains must practice ahimsa, a strict code of nonviolence. Jains believe plants, animals, and even some non-living things (like air and water) have souls, just as humans do. The principle of nonviolence includes doing no harm to humans, plants, animals and nature.

Jainism has its own spiritual leaders and teachers. Jains honour 24 Jinas, or Tirthankaras. Tirthankaras are spiritual leaders who achieved enlightenment and have been liberated from the cycle of rebirth. One of the most influential Jinas was Mahavira. He is considered the 24th and final Jina.

Mahavira says, *"All are my friends. I have no enemies."* According to Mahavira, Nonviolence is the greatest religion. The slogan of Jainism is, "Kill not, cause no pain. Do not injure, abuse, oppress, enslave, insult, torment, torture, or kill any creature or living being."

The teachings of Mahavira include the concept of 12 Bhavnas. Bhavnas mean reflections or thoughts. Maitri Bhavana is the first Bhavna, which focuses on friendship. Maitri Bhavna means "thinking of friendship." We should aim to be a friend to all beings in the universe. By becoming a friend, we refrain from thinking badly of anyone; instead, we strive to make their lives easier.

Lord Mahavira said that we must be a friend to all living beings. The feeling of friendship brings love and respect for others. Friendship initiates a feeling of brotherhood and removes deceit and violence among humans. Maitri Bhavna teaches us to be friends with all, supporting and protecting our fellow human beings with love and affection. Friendship is the only thing that will lead us to be tolerant, forgiving, and caring for one another. It can be seen that if we develop a friendship with all living beings, we will avoid bad karma.

Chapter VI

FRIENDSHIP IN CHRISTIANITY AND ISLAM

"In happiness, in misery, in famine, in pain, in the grave, in heaven, or in hell, who never gives me up is my friend. Is such friendship a joke? A man may have salvation through such friendship,"

– Swami Vivekananda

FRIENDSHIP IN CHRISTIANITY:

Friendship is a highly emphasised relationship in all religions. It holds an important position in Christianity as well. The Holy Bible considers friendship as one of the greatest gifts in human lives. The Bible says, *"Sweet friendships refresh the soul and awaken our hearts with joy, for good friends are like the anointing oil that yields the fragrant incense of God's presence"* (Proverbs 27:9).

Even Jesus Christ declares himself as a friend to his believers. He says, *"You are my friends if you do what I command you… I have called you friend because I have made known to you everything that I have heard from my father"* (John 15:15). This is the key passage in theology for friendship. Jesus said these words to his people because he gave everything to his friends. He shared his knowledge of God, and he gave his own life to them. He proves to be a good friend to all because his love for his friends is unconditional.

45

Christianity lists 3 kinds of friendship. The one we have with our fellow human beings, the friendship we have with ourselves, and the one we have with God are the 3 kinds of friendship.

1. **Friendship With People:**

   The Bible says, *"Love your neighbour as yourself"* (Matthew 22:39). The basis of true friendship is this golden rule. We should treat people with the same love we have for ourselves. *"As you want people to treat you, treat them in the same way"* (Luke 6:31). No one likes to be ill-treated. We like others to love us and respect us for what we are. The one who treats others the way he likes to be treated is a good friend. He does not entertain individual differences and treats his friend the way he treats himself, with love and care. The Bible also says, *"Think of others as more important than yourself"* (Philippians 2:3). Friendship with our fellow beings is characterised by love, respect, and harmony. Considering our friends is important, and prioritising them makes us good friends. Also, knowing and understanding our friends and treating them with utmost respect is the ultimatum in friendship.

2. **Friendship With Self:**

   According to Christianity, we are all *created in the image of God (Genesis 1:27)*. Seeing ourselves with such a notion in our minds will make us love ourselves even more. Self-love is appreciating and supporting our physical, mental, and spiritual growth. When we love ourselves, we would start to care about our well-being. We start to treat ourselves better, not dwelling on bitter experiences but on the betterment of our lives. We will also start to look for good friends to be around us, to guide us and encourage us more in life. Good friends bring happiness and change our perspective of the world. Good friends mean a good life. And a good life starts with self-love.

3. **Friendship with God:**

   We enter into a friendship with God once we become friends with ourselves. Abraham was called the friend of God when he believed

God and did everything in righteousness. God wants us to love others as we love ourselves, and this is the greatest commandment in the Bible. If we follow this commandment, we show God that we love Him and thereby become friends of God.

Certain characteristics are expected to be found in those who believe in Christ and His gospel. The following are 6 characteristics of Christian friendships:

1. **Forgiveness:**

   Friends forgive friends. To Alexander Pope, "to err is human." It is normal for friends to make mistakes. It is inevitable for friends to hurt one another, intentionally or unintentionally. However, forgiving a friend is important to maintaining and sustaining the friendship. The Bible says *it is one's glory to overlook an offence (Proverbs 19:11)*. Forgiving a friend requires patience and maturity. Forgiveness is winning the friendship. Jesus is the true model of forgiveness. Like how He forgave us of our sins, his followers are expected to forgive our friends so that we can *"live in harmony with one another" (Romans 12:16)*

2. **Commitment:**

   The Bible says, *"A friend loves at all times…" (Proverbs 17:17)*. There is no limit to a friend's love. Friends stay devoted to their friendship. Friends stay committed to each other in all trials and tribulations. Christian friends are not only friends, but they are brothers and sisters in Christ. They are a part of the household of faith, and they share a special responsibility with each other. In Christianity, when 2 people are bonded in friendship, they are tied to each other, as in family ties. Hence, commitment is an essential characteristic found to be in Christian friendships.

3. **Discretion:**

   Friends are our human diaries. We hide nothing from our friends. We share everything with our friends that we do not even think of sharing with our parents or siblings. All our secrets are known to our close friends. Good friends are discreet in keeping our secrets as secrets. In Christianity, too, it is no different. It is said in the Bible that *"Whoever goes about slandering reveals secrets, but he who is trustworthy in spirit keeps a thing covered." (Proverbs 11:13)*

So, when friends share their secrets and pray for each other, they pray with discretion. They honour their friends' privacy and stay authentic to their friendship.

4. **Selfless Love:**

Christians represent Christ through their selfless love. They love their friends unconditionally and selflessly. Selfless love in Christian friendships brings extra joy and happiness into each other's lives. Selfless love is possible when we love to help and serve our friends in their adversity and expect nothing in return. Modelling Christ through selfless love is the essence of Christian friendship. Timothy Keller, an American theologian, says, "Spiritual friendship is eagerly helping one another know, serve, love, and resemble God in deeper and deeper ways."

5. **Generosity:**

Generosity is given importance and considered a core value in Christianity. One who loves his friend dearly should be able to be generous to him. Christian friends are called to be free and generous with their money and possessions. The Bible says, *"But if anyone has the world's goods and sees his brother in need, yet closes his eyes against him, how does God's love abide in him?" (1 John 3:17)*

6. **Mutual Edification:**

True friends help each other to grow strong physically, emotionally, and spiritually. They stay with each other not only because it is fun but also because they can edify and build each other up. They share trust and acceptance. They impact one another in being righteous and true to God's words. As it is said in the Bible, *"As iron sharpens iron, so one man sharpens another" (Proverbs 27:17)*; true friends nurture each other to grow more Christlike.

The friend who exhibits these characteristics would make our life blossom with joy, happiness, wisdom, and goodness.

The Bible also talks about bad friends. It is written in the Bible that bad company ruins good morals. There are many examples of bad friends in the Bible who brought destruction and negative impact. One such example is King Ahab, the friend of King Jehoshaphat.

Jehoshaphat was a good king, but he was associated with friends who were bad. King Ahab was one of his bad friends. He brought about the extermination of prophets in Israel. Once, when King Jehoshaphat visited him, King Ahab entertained him well and convinced him to join in the battle against the Philistines in Ramoth-Gilead. So, they both went to Ramoth-Gilead for the battle. Before the battle began, King Ahab said to King Jehoshaphat, "I will disguise myself and go into battle, but you wear your robes." Dressing himself like a soldier, he went to the battle.

Now, the King of Syria commanded his captains to fight with the King of Israel and bring him down. When the captains found King Jehoshaphat in the king's robes, they fought against him. King Jehoshaphat cried out, and the Lord helped him. When the captains found out that he was not King Ahab, the Israel king, they left him and turned back from pursuing him. But a man drew his bow and struck the king of Israel. He got wounded and died at sunset.

Had it not been the Lord who saved King Jehoshaphat, he would have died in the battle. King Ahab tried to fool him, but because King Jehoshaphat was good and righteous, he was saved in the battle.

Another example of a bad friend is Judas Iscariot. He was one disciple among the 12 disciples chosen by Jesus Christ to do full-time ministry. Jesus treated all these 12 men as his disciples, brothers, and friends. So, Judas Iscariot, too, was a friend of Jesus. But Judas Iscariot betrayed Jesus to those who waited to kill Jesus. He went to the enemies of Jesus, the chief priests, and said to them, "What will you give me if I deliver him over to you (Matthew 26:15)?" They paid him 30 pieces of silver. And from that moment, he sought an opportunity to betray Jesus.

While Jesus and His disciples were in the garden of Gethsemane, Judas Iscariot came there with a great crowd with weapons from the chief priests. Judas Iscariot had told them about a sign, saying, "The one I will kiss is the man; seize him," and he came up to Jesus, greeted him, and kissed him. Jesus looked at Judas and said, "Friend, do what you came to do."

The priests and the soldiers came up and laid hands on Jesus, arresting Him. (Reference Matthew 26:14-16, Matthew 26:47-56)

Jesus called Judas a friend because he was able to look past his betrayal and still accept him as his friend. Jesus did not change the relationship from His end but stuck to being a true friend to Judas by accepting and forgiving him.

Jesus also had good friends. He had a close friendship with Mary, Martha, and Lazarus (Luke 10:38–42 and John 11:1–46). Mary, Martha, and their brother Lazarus were faithful followers of Jesus.

One day, Lazarus became seriously ill, and Mary and Martha were worried. They sent a message to Jesus, hoping He would cure Lazarus' sickness. But Jesus was with his disciples in Peraea.

When Jesus received the message of Lazarus' sickness, he said, "This sickness is not unto death, but for the glory of God, that the Son of God might be glorified thereby." He stayed in Peraea for 2 more days. Then he said to his disciples, "Let us go into Judaea again." However, his disciples were worried about His returning to Judaea, and they tried to persuade Him not to go because the people in Judaea were threatening to stone Him, as Jesus was claiming to be the Son of God. Therefore, the disciples were afraid to go to Judaea.

Jesus, who loved Lazarus so much, said, "Our friend Lazarus sleepeth; but I go, that I may awake him out of sleep." When the disciples could not understand what he meant, Jesus said plainly, "Lazarus is dead."

Jesus and His disciples visited Lazarus' place and found out Lazarus had laid in the tomb for 4 days. His sisters were mourning his death. Seeing Mary and her friends weeping, Jesus felt sad and troubled. When they saw Jesus, Martha cried and said, "Lord, if thou hadst been here, my brother would not have died." Then Martha showed her great faith by adding, "But I know that even now, whatsoever thou wilt ask of God, God will give it thee." To her, Jesus said, "Thy brother shall rise again."

They walked to Lazarus's tomb, and there Jesus wept. The people who saw Jesus weeping said, "Behold how [Jesus] loved him!"

The tomb was covered with a big stone. When Jesus asked to take the stone away, Martha hesitated, saying, "Lord, by this time, he stinketh: for he has been dead 4 days." Jesus turned to her and said, "Said I not unto thee, that if thou wouldest believe, thou shouldest see the glory of God?"

Then, the people rolled away the stone. Jesus lifted his eyes up and prayed. Then he cried with a loud voice, "Lazarus, come forth." The dead Lazarus, still wrapped in his grave clothes, came forth. Jesus asked the people to unwind the cloth that covered Lazarus. When they did so, they saw Lazarus was very much alive. The people were amazed. Thus, Jesus performed a miracle for his dear friend, Lazarus.

The Bible consists of many such good friends' stories. It also talks about fair-weather friends. Job's story in the book of Job is an example of such fair-weather friendship.

The job was a righteous man. He had a wife, sons, daughters, servants, and large herds of livestock. He was righteous and faithful to God. When Satan pointed out to God that only because of his riches he is being faithful, God decided to allow Satan to test Job in order to prove to Satan that a righteous man would still be faithful in all circumstances. During the test, Job lost all his riches. He even lost his sons and daughters, and only his wife was left behind. Job also felt sick with boils and sores all over his body. He was about as low as a man can get on this Earth. But in all this, Job did not sin or speak against God.

His 3 close friends, Eliphaz, Bildad, and Zophar, heard of his affliction, and they came to see him. They sat with him for 7 days and nights and said nothing, just mourned with him. After 7 days of mourning, they started to speak to him. They began a long, miserable debate about the reasons for Job's suffering. They told Job that it was his fault that he was suffering. Job was confused and frustrated because he knew God was just, but he also knew that he had done no sin. When his friends kept attacking him and insisted that his suffering was his own doing, Job called out to God for proof. Eventually, God rebuked the friends and blessed Job even more than before.

In the *Book of Job*, it is mentioned more than once that Job was a righteous man, but his friends apparently did not know and understand Job and his righteousness. If they had spent the time to really get to know him, they would have believed and trusted Job. They would have spoken words of comfort to him.

Friendship is the resource of faith and ethics for Christians. In the Bible, a "friend" is immediately understood as "one who loves." Jesus' act of giving his own life shows his loyalty and compassion in friendship. He proved himself to be a model of true friendship so that we understand friendship is loving and being there for one another, no matter what challenges life throws at us.

FRIENDSHIP IN ISLAM:

In Islam, the Holy Prophet explains the impact of friends, saying, "Man is influenced by the faith of his friends. Therefore, be careful of whom you befriend." Friends can be the influencers of our life. "Tell me your friends, and I'll tell you who you are," is a popular Assyrian Proverb. This proverb suggests not only that like minds stick together but also how friends can influence the choices of our life.

According to Islam, friendship is not only a social construct but a religiously significant relationship. Islam also asks us to keep friends that bring us closer to Allah and to make sure we treat them well.

The Quran teaches Muslims to "help one another in good deeds, and do not help one another in mischief." It emphasises the concept of friendship because maintaining good friendships helps in shaping one's life and influences the spiritual path chosen in life.

Islam attaches great emphasis to the choice of a friend to be selected in life. True friendship is based on an ethical and spiritual foundation. "Your best friend is the one who, when you see him, reminds you of Allah; when you speak to him, your knowledge increases, and his actions remind you of the hereafter," says Al-Muhasibi, the founder of the Baghdad School of Islamic philosophy.

The Holy Prophet says, "Man is influenced by the faith of his friends. Therefore, be careful of whom you befriend." Friendship can influence and affect many aspects of our lives. Sayyid Mujtaba Musavi Lari, in his book Ethics and Spiritual Growth, says, "One must know his/her inadequacies and weak points, his/her ideas, feelings, dislikes, and infirmities. Ultimately, one must discover the human merits and desirable qualities that he/she carries in the depth of his/her spirit so that one may benefit from his/her outstanding virtues." Therefore, for the great good or bad influences friends can have on the characters and personality of each other, it is important for every man of reason to choose friends characterised by good mannerisms and behaviour.

CHARACTERISTICS OF A GOOD FRIEND:

According to Islam, the following are some of the characteristics to be looked for in a friend:

- Intelligence,

- Faith,

- Honesty,

- Uprightness and,

- Being well-mannered.

A friend who is intelligent enough to guide and mentor his friends is considered to be a true friend. One who mentors a friend will have faith in what he believes and make sure his friends walk in the right path like him. He will be honest with his friends and will not encourage the things that are misguiding them. The one who betrays his friends is unworthy of friendship.

In accordance with some narrations (Hadiths), a true friend will,

- Respect his friends without judging their personalities.

- Give material support when they are in need.

- Guide them when they are in need of counsel.

- Protect their secrets.

- Forgive their mistakes.

- Visit them in their sickness.

- Participate in their joys and sorrows.

Friends are integral parts of our social life, and the one who fails to meet the above criteria may lead to deplorable consequences, bringing regret and pain.

The Quran classifies friends as follows:

1. **SADDIQUE** - The one who is termed as Saddique is a genuine friend. He is a friend for our well-being. He does not look for any benefit from us. He is the one who will never give up on us, even when we make mistakes. He always stays in touch with us throughout his lifetime.

2. **SAHIB** - Sahib is the person who is acquainted with us. He is concerned about us and tries to help us to the best of his ability.

3. **WALEJA** - A friend who is a business partner is termed as Waleja. He is involved in our business and sees to it that we do not lose any money in the business. He is an honest and trustworthy person and will remain so all his life.

4. **BITA'ANA** - A friend who is our confidante and keeps our secrets within himself is called Bita'ana.

5. **QAREEN** - Qareen is a friend with whom we have a lot in common. He is a friend with the same likes and dislikes as us. He thinks and acts in the same way.

6. **KHALEEL** - Khaleel is a friend who always thinks about us even when we are not with him. He loves us dearly and is always ready to do anything for us.

7. **RAFEEQ** - A friend with whom we feel relaxed and get comfort in his company is called Rafeeq.

8. **KHAZOUL** – Khazoul is a friend who only pretends to befriend. He remains with us only for his convenience. He disappears when we are in trouble. He is a deceitful friend.

9. **KHADAN** – Khadan is a kind of friendship between girls and boys, which is strongly prohibited in Islam.

Islam advises keeping away from friends who make us forget to pray. The Quran says, *"And (remember) the day when the unjust one shall bite his hands, saying: O! Would that I had taken away with the Messenger! O woe is me! Would that I had not taken such a one for a friend! Certainly, he led me astray from the reminder after it had come to me. Ah! The Evil One is but a traitor to man!" (25:27-29).*

This verse clearly says that Allah Almighty approves of friendship. Friendship is an important relationship for Muslims. It also advises following the path of righteousness together as friends in order to receive paradise after their death. One who complains about their friends and laments upon them will only go to hell.

"And (as for) the believing men and the believing women, they are guardians of each other. They enjoin good, forbid evil, keep up prayer, pay the poor rate, and obey Allah and His Messenger. (As for) these, Allah will show mercy to them; surely, Allah is Mighty, Wise." (9:71)

It is imperative that a Muslim has righteous friends. Those who are pious would remain friends with each other. Therefore, one should be friends with someone who is pious and righteous. Also, the pious men should fulfil all the obligations of Islam. He must follow the instructions of Allah Almighty and the Sunnah of Prophet Muhammad in every aspect of their life to be considered a good friend.

The Quran talks about hypocritical friends, too.

"The hypocritical men and the hypocritical women are all alike; they enjoin evil, forbid good, and withhold their hands; they have forsaken Allah, so He has forsaken them; surely the hypocrites are the transgressors." (9:67)

Friends can be evil and hypocrites, too. They pretend to be a friend but have evil thoughts about us. They forget Allah and His instructions. A Muslim should not befriend such people, as their friendship only leads to downfall and destruction.

Imam Sajjad said to his honourable son, Imam Baqir, to avoid 5 people in life. It is narrated in the book of Usul al-Kafi. The 5 people mentioned are:

1. Liars:

    A friend who is truthful in nature can only be called a true friend. The one who lies should not be considered a friend because he can deceive us at times in life. A liar is like a mirage, which deceives us by showing the far close to us and taking the close far from us. Like in any other religion, lying is a sin in Islam.

2. Transgressor:

    A transgressor is a betrayer who would violate the trust of a friend. They do not obey the obligation in Islam; rather, they would be ready to betray their friends for even a morsel of food.

3. Stingy person:

    A stingy person would refuse to help his friend in his time of need. It is best not to befriend a stingy person.

4. Stupid:

    One should avoid the companionship of a stupid person because, in his stupidity, he would bring harm to his friend. He does not know how to tackle difficult situations, and even though he wants to help, he acts stupidly and brings danger to his companion.

5.   One who has no kin:

One should avoid the companionship of a person who has cut off his ties of kinship because it is written in the Quran that he has gone away from the mercy of Allah. The Quran says, *"But if you held command, you were sure to make mischief in the land and cut off the ties of kinship! Those it is whom Allah has cursed, so He has made them deaf and blinded their eyes."*

Allah has said: *"And those who break the covenant of Allah after its confirmation, and cut asunder that which Allah has ordered to be joined, and make mischief in the land; (as for) those, upon them, shall be a curse, and they shall have the evil (issue) of the abode."*

He has also said: *"Who break the covenant of Allah after its confirmation and cut asunder what Allah has ordered to be joined, and make mischief in the land; these, it is, that are the losers"* (Selection taken from *Forty Hadiths*, vol. 3, by Sayyid Hashim Rasouli Mahallati)

Being friends with the righteous ones helps us in following the path of righteousness. A scholar has said: "To seal a friendship for Allah's sake indicates the obligation of establishing relationships of love and trust for His sake; this is a friendship for the sake of Allah. It also indicates that simple affection is not enough here; indeed, what is meant is a love based upon alliance. This entails assistance, honour, and respect. It means being with those whom you love, both in word and deed."

An incident in the Quran tells how important it is to have a righteous friend.

"A person visited his brother in another town, and God sent an angel to wait for him on his way." The angel said, "Where do you intend to go?" The man answered, "I intend to go to my brother in this town." The angel said, "Have you done any favour to him, the repayment of which you intend to get?" He said, "No, I love him for the sake of God, the Exalted and Glorious." Thereupon, the angel said, "I am a messenger to you from God to inform you that God loves you as you love him."

Iman Ali bin Abi Thalib said, "Find friends for yourself from among your coreligionist brethren since they are the treasures of this world and also the next world."

In Islam, a true friend is like a treasure, not only in this world but also in the afterlife. Good friends make us happy even in the afterlife.

Chapter VII

FRIENDSHIP IN WORLD HISTORY

The language of friendship is not words, but meanings

– Henry David Thoreau

Long-lasting friendships are a treasure in life. Every human being deserves long-lasting friendships in their life. There is no other valuable treasure in life to be cherished other than a true friend. True friends are those who come into our lives like a miracle and change our whole perspective about life. Some friends may grow apart, but true friends come farther with us than expected.

Many of the greatest historical personalities have enjoyed such long-lasting friendships in their lives. Their legendary friendships inspire us and make us appreciate the concept of friendships even more. Let's look at such popular friendships that have made a mark in our world history.

1. MARK TWAIN AND HELEN KELLER

"Walking with a friend in the dark is better than walking alone in the light," said Helen Keller. For over a decade, Keller was friends with Mark Twain, the father of American literature. He was also a mentor to her. "Mark Twain has his own way of thinking, saying, and doing everything. I can feel the twinkle of his eye in his handshake. Even while he utters his cynical wisdom in an indescribably droll voice, he makes you feel that his heart is a tender Iliad of human sympathy," she wrote.

Samuel Clemens, also known as Mark Twain, and Helen Keller met in 1895 at a party held in her honour by the editor Laurence Hutton in New York City. Keller was only 14 at the time. Despite the age difference, they struck up a good friendship, which they maintained for a long time. Twain wrote in his autobiography, "Without touching anything, and without seeing anything, obviously, and without hearing anything, she seemed to quite well recognise the character of her surroundings. She said, 'Oh, the books, the books, so many, many books. How lovely!"

In a handshake, Keller knew that Twain was going to be her friend. At that party, Twain and Keller discovered a shared love of learning and laughter. "I told her a long story, which she interrupted all along and in the right places, with cackles, chuckles, and carefree bursts of laughter," Twain recalled.

Keller was already a fan of Twain's works. After being treated as an equal by him, Keller found him to be a good friend, and until his death, they remained friends.

Twain was the one who helped her to go to college at Radcliffe. She was the first deaf and blind person in the world to earn a Bachelor of Arts degree in 1904. She learnt to read English, French, German, and Latin in braille and went on to become practically as world-famous as her dear friend, writing prolifically and lecturing across the country and around the world.

Keller shared some of the fond memories of her friend Twain in her autobiographical book, which she published in 1929. About Twain, she writes,

"There are writers who belong to the history of their nation's literature. Mark Twain is one of them. When we think of great Americans, we think of him. He incorporated the age he lived in. To me, he symbolises the pioneer qualities—the large, free, unconventional, humorous point of view of men who sail new seas and blaze new trails through the wilderness."

Keller proved to be a good friend to Mark Twain by consoling him after the death of his beloved wife, Olivia, in 1904. She was a shoulder to lean on when Twain was mourning for his wife. She considered Twain as her good friend because he treated her as an equal and like a competent human being. As for Twain, he was always filled with wonder when he saw her. He admired her knowledge, which she acquired because of being shut off from all distractions. He once said, "If I could have been deaf, dumb, and blind, I also might have arrived at something."

2. THOMAS EDISON AND HENRY FORD

Thomas Edison and Henry Ford shared a genuine friendship in their lifetime. They were both iconic inventors. Thomas Edison's inventions, like the phonograph, light bulb, and carbon microphone, changed the world tremendously. The American industrialist Henry Ford's inventions are no less.

They both met for a short time at a convention, and that brief encounter led to a life-long friendship, which made them buy vacation homes together in later days.

Henry Ford met Thomas Edison in 1896 at the convention of the Association of Edison Illuminating Companies in New York. Since Ford's childhood, he had been a fan of Edison. So, when he met him at the convention, he took some candid shots of him. Then, he was introduced to Edison as the inventor of a cart powered by a gasoline-powered engine. Edison was impressed with Ford's work, and he said, "Your car is self-contained – carries its own power plant – no fire, no boiler, no smoke, and no steam. You have the thing. Keep at it."

This encounter with Edison left a strong impression on Ford's mind. He started to work on his invention. Meanwhile, they both had grown fond of each other and had started to exchange birthday messages. Ford sent a greeting to Edison in 1915 as thousand congratulations" and he received a thank-you message that opened with "My dear Mr. Ford," and ended with "Yours very truly."

When Ford asked Edison to collaborate with him on making an electric car, Edison asked him to build a battery used in cars. Ford agreed and lent him the $700,000 to fund the car battery. Edison was not able to deliver the battery as he promised. Ford did not ask him about it. When he found out that the battery did not work, he put the contract up for a re-bid and gave it to another company. Edison did not protest this. Their business relationship did not affect their friendship in any way. Ford supported Edison financially throughout his life. He gave Edison a loan of $100,000 when his factory burnt down. For Edison's 82nd birthday, Ford gifted him $5 million to establish an endowment for his museum's collection of Edison and to establish a technical school in Edison's name.

Till today, Ford's estate, "The Mangoes," is next to Edison's "Seminole Lodge." A non-profit organisation called "The Thomas Edison & Henry Ford Winter Estates" was started in 2003 to protect and preserve the sites. The estates remain one of the popular historical attractions in southwest Florida. They stand as proof of the greatest friendship between 2 great businessmen who stayed friends until their last breath.

3. C.S. LEWIS AND J.R.R. TOLKIEN

There was a famous friendship between 2 eminent authors over 50 years ago. They had written famous books like *The Hobbit, The Lord of the Rings*, and *The Chronicles of Narnia series*. They were none other than J.R.R. Tolkien and C.S. Lewis.

Tolkien was born in Bloemfontein, South Africa in 1892. C.S. Lewis was born in Belfast, United Kingdom, in 1898. Initially, they were teaching English at Oxford University. They both lived ordinary lives like any tutors, spending their time researching and lecturing. They met in 1926 when they both came to attend a teachers' meeting at Merton College. They immediately became friends with each other. Tolkien was a Christian, and Lewis was not. They both talked about religion and myth. Lewis realised that the truth found in all the world's stories pointed to the real truth found in the Bible and became a steadfast Christian. He then brought hope and moral inspiration to England during World War II.

C.S. Lewis wrote about their first meeting in his diary: "[Tolkien has] no harm in him: only needs a smack or so." They shared many common interests, like stories, myths, and fantasies. They had no car, so they walked everywhere in town. They made time to meet every week with their other friends, and they called their informal club 'The Inklings.' They read their writings there and discussed them. The club helped to improve their literary works.

C.S. Lewis and Tolkien had nicknames for each other. Tolkien called Lewis "Jack," and Lewis called Tolkien "Tollers." They made fun of each other's works. Lewis thought Tolkien's writings were long and complicated, and Tolkien thought Lewis's allegory was too simple. They were critics of each other, but they both supported them with constructive criticism. It was C.S. Lewis who encouraged J.R.R. Tolkien to write *The Lord of the Rings*.

C.S. Lewis and J.R.R. Tolkien served as second lieutenants in World War I and lost their closest friends in combat. The Great War left deep scars in their lives. Lewis reported suffering from troubling dreams about the war for years after his service had ended. Despite the horrors they faced, both remained idealistic. Instead of writing bitter novels, they wrote concepts that honoured heroism and virtue. They borrowed concepts from the great epic stories and ignited the imaginations of children and adults by writing incredible works.

Without this friendship, they would not have reached the zenith in the literary world. Though the last decade of their lives was spent on unspoken resentments, they were good friends in the beginning, which made them leave indelible impressions on English literature.

C.S. Lewis died from kidney failure on 22nd November 1963. After hearing of his former friend's passing, Tolkien penned a letter to his daughter, Priscilla, "This feels like an axe blow near the roots. Very sad that we should have been so separated in the last years, but our time of close communion endured in memory for both of us."

4. ELLA FITZGERALD AND MARILYN MONROE

Marilyn Monroe and Ella Fitzgerald were close friends. In an interview, when Monroe was asked who her favourite singer was, she answered, "Well, my very favourite person, and I love her as a person as well as a singer; I think she's the greatest, and that's Ella Fitzgerald."

They both met in November 1954 in Los Angeles where Fitzgerald was performing in a concert. Monroe spent hours listening to her music. Their friendship began at the concert. They had a lot in common. They had unhappy childhoods and unsuccessful marriages. Unlike Ella Fitzgerald, Monroe was open about her life in public.

Once, when Fitzgerald mentioned, "I know I make a lot of money at the jazz clubs I play, but I sure wish I could play at one of those fancy places," Marilyn Monroe stepped in and helped her to get a slot at Mocambo, a famous L.A. nightclub.

In those days, African Americans were not allowed to perform in the famous nightclubs. When Marilyn Monroe asked the club owner of Mocambo, he claimed Fitzgerald lacked the glamour to draw crowds. However, Monroe proposed a deal to him that if he hired Fitzgerald, she promised she would sit at the front of the house every night and bring along other famous faces to his club. The club owner accepted the deal, and since that moment, Ella Fitzgerald's career started to climb up the career ladder.

"I owe Marilyn Monroe a real debt... she was an unusual woman - a little ahead of her times. And she didn't know it," said Ella

Fitzgerald. She remembered, "After that, I never had to play a small jazz club again."

Though Ella Fitzgerald was allowed to sing in the famous clubs, she was not allowed to enter through the main entrance. When Marilyn went to see her friend's performance, she witnessed Ella being led away from the main entrance and became furious at this racist treatment. Marilyn Monroe refused to go inside the club unless Ella was allowed to use the main entrance. From that day, no one dared to make Ella use the side door to enter the clubs. She became one of the most influential jazz singers.

Their friendship was going strong, but when Monroe was struggling with drug addiction, it drifted apart from time to time. Fitzgerald preferred to stay away from drugs and liked to keep her life quiet. Despite the differences, they supported each other until Monroe passed away at the young age of 36 in 1962.

5. KUYILI AND QUEEN VELU NACHIYAR

Velu Nachiyar and Kuyili are the 2 women who took down the British, 85 years before, in the year 1857.

Velu Nachiyar was the first queen from India to bravely rebel against the British forces. She was married to Muthuvaduganathaperiya Udaiyathevar, the king of Sivagangai.

In 1772, Muthuvaduganathaperiya Udaiyathevar, the second king of Sivaganga, was embroiled in a war with the Nawab of Arcot because he refused to yield to his demands. In the battle, Muthuvaduganathaperiya Udaiyathevar lost his life, and the invading British army entered the Sivaganga district. They plundered Kalaiyar Koil and collected jewels worth 50,000 pagodas.

Velu Nachiyar, who was a woman of rare intellect and well-known for her bravery, did not surrender to the British but fled with her daughter to the neighbouring kingdom. However, as a fugitive queen, she knew it was unwise to fight against the British single-handedly. So, she remained in hiding at Virupachi for 8 long years. She was determined to take vengeance against the British and was waiting patiently for the right opportunity.

During her years in hiding, she managed to arrange a huge army that included many women warriors. She trained her warriors to perfection. The army commander was Kuyili, who was the bravest and the ablest of all women warriors.

Kuyili was born at Kudanchavadi near Sivagangai. She had an unconditional love for her motherland and was determined to sacrifice her own life if needed.

Velu Nachiyar and her army drew up a plan. They zeroed in on a person from the south who already had a notorious past with both the Nawab and the British. His name was Hyder Ali. Impressed with the queen's unwavering resolve against British rule, he offered to help her in her plans. In 1780, they geared up for a war against the British. They encountered the enemy troops and defeated them at 3 places: Madurai, Thirubhuvanam, and Kalaiyarkoil.

When they decided to march towards Sivaganagi to recapture the fort, they were informed by the spy that the British were ready with heavy guns and ammunition which could kill them from a long-distance. If only they could destroy the enemy's ammunition and guns, they could attain victory. But the ammunition and the guns were kept in a warehouse near Raja Rajeshwari temple. When they were clueless about how to destroy the warehouse, Kuyili stepped in. She devised a plan and discussed it with the queen. She undertook complete responsibility by volunteering for the task of bringing down the British warehouse where they had kept all their ammunition. She divided the Udayal Padai wing into groups. They planned to strike the British after the third round of worship on Vijayadasami day.

After the worship ended and the devotees left the temple, the women's army attacked the British soldiers. The British soldiers rushed to the warehouse to fetch their ammunition to counter the army of Velu Nachiyar. At that moment, Kuyili hurried towards the deity and poured a pot of ghee over herself. She also grabbed the ghee oil lamp and hurried towards the warehouse.

The British soldiers, who were rushing towards the warehouse, suddenly stopped as they realised what was going to happen. In no time, the warehouse exploded. Kuyili had turned into a human bomb by lighting herself in the warehouse. She turned into ashes in no time. She sacrificed herself for her motherland by destroying the warehouse of guns and ammunition of the British forces.

Then, in the battle that ensued between the British and Velu Nachiyar's army, the British lost. Captain Benjour, who was leading the British forces, pleaded for his life to the queen and promised that the British would never step inside the Sivagangai Kingdom again. Velu Nachiyar set him free and let him go.

She then ruled the kingdom for over a decade until her death in 1796.

If not for Kuyili, who sacrificed her life as the first human bomber of India, they would not have won the battle and got back their kingdom again. Her love for the motherland and her admiration for the queen made her lose her own life. Thus, she proved to be a trustworthy friend of Queen Velu Nachiyar.

6. JADUNATH SARKAR, G.S. SARDESAI, AND RAGHUBIR SINH

A friend's group of 3 made the writing of Indian history energetic. The remarkable friends' group consists of 3 historians: Jadunath Sarkar, G.S. Sardesai, and Raghubir Sinh.

Since we deserved the name of friends,

And thy effect so lives in me,

A part of mine may live in thee.

And move thee on to nobler ends.

These are the lines quoted by Jadunath Sarkar in a letter written to G.S. Sardesai in Kamshet. These lines are from the poem "In Memoriam" by Alfred Lord Tennyson.

The friendship between Jadunath Sarkar and G.S. Sardesai had extended over half a century. It began in 1904 when both were relatively obscure scholars, and the friendship continued when both were regarded as sage historian scholars of their times.

Jadunath Sarkar and G.S. Sardesai were introduced to each other by Gopal Rao Deodhar, who suggested that their association would be mutually beneficial: to Sarkar for Maratha documents and to Sardesai for Persian and Mughal sources. Following the introduction, Sardesai received a letter from Sarkar, in which he said:

"Sometime in the year 1904, a letter in an unknown handwriting, indicating vigour and precision, and with contents securely formal and business-like, took me by surprise at Baroda. The name of the writer did not solve the mystery as I had not, until then, heard of him."

Their first correspondence became "the pledge of future cooperation between the Mughal and Maratha."

Sarkar and Sardesai first met in 1909 at a Maratha Literary Conference held in Baroda. Sardesai was the secretary of the conference. He had the long-sought opportunity to meet Jadunath Sarkar after 4 years of acquaintance through correspondence. They both exchanged letters after their first meeting, which described the time spent together. They met once every year afterwards for the next 4 decades, and in between those meetings, Sardesai wrote, "We have built a historic bridge of letters, concealed as yet from any fifth eye." The frailty of old age prevented meetings thereafter, but the correspondence continued until Sarkar's death.

The third figure in this triad is Maharajkumar Raghubir Sinh, an heir to the throne of the small princely state of Sitamau in Central

India. He wanted to conduct serious historical research, and his quest brought Sinh and Sarkar together. Sarkar wrote to Raghubir Sinh in September 1933, "I am very glad indeed to learn that you intend to continue your historical research. It will be no trouble to me, but a pleasure rather, to render you any assistance in my power." Sinh became Sarkar's favourite student. They became friends after he submitted a thesis, 'Malwa in Transition or a Century of Anarchy (1698-1766),' to Agra University.

Through his mentor, Sarkar, Sinh was drawn to Sardesai and became an equal participant in the endeavours of his seniors. The pursuits of the trio inevitably linked with a particularly fraught aspect of Indian historiography. As his mentors aged and their influence declined, he was to emerge as the person who would carry their legacy forward and complete the unfinished tasks.

This little group of friends shared research interests, a commitment to writing history, and a close, supportive friendship. They wrote letters to each other and decided to retain their letters. Their correspondence concentrated primarily on the seventeenth and eighteenth centuries as each scholar explored their personal interests. Raghubir Sinh kept all the letters Sarkar and Sardesai wrote to him for a quarter of a century, from about 1933 to 1959.

There was a unifying theme in all the letters, but there are other themes as well: advancing historical scholarship through mutual support, friendship, and loyalty.

The friendship between this trio and the little squad proved that true friendships add value to our lives. Having a like-minded friend, sharing the same interests, and important core values is crucial to having a happier, healthier mental state.

7. **BAL GANGADHAR TILAK AND MOHAMMED ALI JINNAH**

Lokmanya Bal Gangadhar Tilak and Mohammed Ali Jinnah were one of the most intriguing political relationships in the history of India.

Tilak was a Hindu communalist. He was born on 23 July 1856 in the coastal town of Ratnagiri in the Konkan region of Maharashtra. He had a passion for politics. His mission was to attain India's complete independence from British rule. To popularise his mission, he established 2 newspapers, Kesari (in Marathi, the native language of Maharashtra) and Mahratta (in English). These newspapers caught the attention of the British and earned him the ire of the colonial administration.

He was arrested twice by the British on charges of sedition. They arrested him first in 1897 and then in 1908 when he was banished to Burma for 6 years. His banishment provoked the first-ever political strike by the working class. The textile workers of Bombay (Hindus of all castes, as well as Muslims) struck work for 6 days, one day for every year of the sentence.

Tilak was fearless and determined to fulfil his mission. He roared like a lion in the Bombay High Court, "Swaraj is my birthright, and I shall have it." When the judge asked him if he had anything to say before the sentence was pronounced, he audaciously replied, "All I wish to say is that, in spite of the verdict of the jury, I maintain my innocence. There are higher powers that rule the destiny of men and nations. It may be the will of providence that the cause I represent may prosper by suffering rather than by remaining free."

These inspiring words were etched on a marble plaque in courtroom no. 46 at Bombay High Court. Such was his determination and valour.

Tilak was convinced that the unity between Hindu and Muslim communities was necessary for India's liberation and future progress. He affirmed that Indian nationalism is 'composite.' He meant that Hindus and Muslims were equals. Tilak wrote in Kesari: "When Hindus and Muslims jointly ask for Swarajya from a common platform, the British bureaucracy has to realise that its days are numbered."

On the other hand, Jinnah was a Muslim communalist. He was the most promising young lawyer and nationalist Muslim politician in India in the first 2 decades of the last century. He was also an active member of both the Congress and the Muslim League.

The friendship between Jinnah and Tilak developed when both the Indian National Congress and the All-India Muslim League jointly demanded from the British self-rule for Indians. Gopal Krishna Gokhale, Tilak's mentor and the respected leader of the "moderate" faction of the Congress, described Jinnah as "an ambassador of Hindu-Muslim unity." Jinnah and Tilak, despite the differences in their religious practices, became close friends.

Jinnah gave a speech at a public meeting in Shantaram Chawl. There, he praised Tilak as "no man was more fitted to voice the opinions of the democracy here to the English people than Mr Tilak who had devoted his whole life to the cause of his country. Let it be quite clear," he said, "that the demand for the immediate step towards the establishment of the Home Rule was the united demand of the people. It was the birthright of every man, and that was the principle of self-determination."

Tilak gave a rousing call for Indian unity in the same meeting: "Stand by us, now and ever, like men, resolute men, against the temptation that would be offered by the [British] bureaucracy. Accept no compromise, no barter, no change in the matter. If you accept it, we all will be humiliated and laughed at. The bureaucracy might try to create a split among us. Be careful, attentive, and resolute to stand by the Congress Scheme."

Jinnah strongly believed in the idea of the "union of the 2 great communities in India." When he gave a speech at Anjuman-i-Islam on January 20, 1913, he said it was a necessity for the Hindus and Muslims "to combine in one harmonious union for the common good."

Tilak-Jinnah's comradeship symbolised Hindu-Muslim solidarity for India's freedom. They are the ones responsible for strengthening the unity of today's multi-faith India and for promoting harmony in our multi-community society.

A.G. Noorani, a prolific scholar, wrote a book about their comradeship. In his book *Jinnah and Tilak: Comrades in the Freedom Struggle,*' he writes: "Theirs was not what is known as 'drawing room politics.' They plunged deep into mass politics."

Kanji Dwarkadas, a close friend of Jinnah in Bombay, said, "The 2 great political centres in Bombay at that time (c. 1916) were Sardar Griha, where Tilak lived, and Jinnah's chambers in the High Court. All political roads led to these 2 places for organisation, consultation, and decision."

Mohammed Ali Currim Chagla, the great jurist, served as Chief Justice of the Bombay High Court from 1948 to 1958. He worked in Jinnah's chamber when he was a young lawyer. Tilak was his childhood hero. He also idolised Jinnah and became a member of the Muslim League. He writes: "I might mention here that during my long association with him, I found that Jinnah always showed the greatest respect and regard for Tilak. Even when he was in the process of changing his political stand and becoming more and more communal, I never remember him ever saying anything derogatory of Tilak. Two persons in public life for whom Jinnah showed the greatest respect were Gokhale and Tilak. He had hard and harsh things to say about Gandhiji, Nehru, and others, but as far as Gokhale and Tilak were concerned, Jinnah had the most profound admiration and respect for them and for their views. It is surprising that there should have been so much in common between Jinnah and Tilak. I understand that Jinnah's regard for Tilak was reciprocated by Tilak. Jinnah told me that when as a junior he was reading in the chamber of Lowndes–Sir George Lowndes, who afterwards became a member of the Viceroy's Legislative Council, and later still a member of the Privy Council–Lowndes' opinion was once sought regarding some speech that Tilak had delivered. There was going to be a conference, and Lowndes asked Jinnah whether he had read the brief and what he thought about it. Jinnah replied that he had not touched the brief and would not look at it as he wanted to keep himself free to criticise the government for prosecuting a great patriot like Tilak. Jinnah said that Lowndes was amused at the indignation and enthusiasm of his young junior."

The valorous efforts made by these far-sighted leaders, who belonged to 2 different communities, for the reconciliation of differences are remarkable. They worked together towards the construction of a future of amicable co-existence in Hindu-Muslim amity and good neighbourliness in India-Pakistan.

Tilak died of illness in Bombay on August 1, 1920. The funeral at Chowpatty Beach was attended by over a million people. Gandhi wrote in his newspaper Young India: "A giant among men has fallen. The voice of the lion is hushed... he knew no religion but the love of his country… he had an iron will, which he used for his country. His life was an open book. His private life was spotlessly clean. No man preached the gospel of swaraj (freedom) with the consistency and the insistence of the Lokamanya (an honorific which means a leader respected by the people)."

Jinnah, in his tribute, wrote: "Mr Tilak rendered yeoman services to the country and played a very important part in bringing about the Hindu-Muslim unity, which ultimately resulted in the Lucknow Pact in 1916."

8. SRINIVASA RAMANUJAN AND GODFREY HAROLD HARDY

This is the story of a close friendship that blossomed between 2 great mathematicians.

Ramanujan, India's great mathematician, passed his matriculation exam in the year 1903. Since he concentrated only on mathematics, he did not progress in academics. He became a clerk in the Madras Post Trust office in 1912. He was obsessed with numbers and kept working on fractions, divergent series, elliptic integrals, hypergeometric series, and the distribution of primes. He was desperate to gain recognition from the mathematicians in England. So, he wrote a long letter about his discoveries and sent it to Godfrey Harold Hardy, the Cambridge mathematician. This is how their friendship began, and the letter changed both of their lives.

Hardy was an outstanding mathematician and also a wonderful teacher. He was eager to nurture talents. When he received the letter from Ramanujan, he discussed it with another great mathematician, Littlewood. They could prove some of the claims in the letter, but they found it impossible to resolve many. After much reviewing of the letter, they were convinced that Ramanujan was a genius. So, Hardy wrote an encouraging reply to Ramanujan, and that paved the way for many such exchanges of letters.

Hardy found Ramanujan to be exceptional in mathematics. However, he lacked the basic tools of the trade of a professional mathematician. Hardy decided to tutor him so that he would have a solid foundation in mathematics. He invited Ramanujan to Cambridge University to pursue his studies.

But in those days, Brahmins were not allowed to cross the ocean. Ramanujan's mother did not entertain the idea of Ramanujan leaving the country. After much pleading, Ramanujan got his mother's permission in 1914.

Hardy immediately asked E.H. Neville, a student of Trinity College, to secure Ramanujan a scholarship from the University of Madras while he was on a trip to Madras. Neville wrote in a letter to the university that "the discovery of the genius of S. Ramanujan of Madras promises to be the most interesting event of our time in the mathematical world…"

Ramanujan sailed for England in the company of Neville and arrived in Cambridge in April 1914. Hardy cared for Ramanujan and mentored him. He taught him mathematics without breaking his confidence. To quote Hardy, "The limitations of his knowledge were as startling as its profundity. Here was a man who could work out modular equations and theorems of complex multiplication to orders unheard of, whose mastery of continued fractions was, on the formal side at any rate, beyond that of any mathematician in the world... It was impossible to ask such a man to submit to systematic instruction and try to learn mathematics from the beginning once more. On the other hand, there were things of which it was impossible that he would remain in ignorance... so I had to try to teach him, and in a measure, I succeeded, though I obviously learnt from him much more than he learnt from me."

Ramanujan graduated with a BA and published many excellent papers on mathematics. But in 1917, he fell ill. When he recovered from his illness in 1919, he decided to return to India. He wrote a letter to Hardy in February 1920, which contained some examples of his latest discovery: mock theta functions. They turned out to be very important because the modular forms in mathematics had a major conjecture of applications to elliptic curves, Borcherds products, Eichler cohomology, and Galois representations – and the nature of black holes.

Sadly, Ramanujan, aged just 32, passed away on April 26, 1920. He benefited only for a short time from his fellowship of the Royal Society and fellowship of Trinity.

Hardy lived on for some 27 years after Ramanujan's death. He died at the ripe old age of 70. When he was asked about his relationship with Ramanujan and his contribution to mathematics, he unhesitatingly honoured Ramanujan and commented on their collaboration as the only romantic incident in his life.

It is only because of the Cambridge mathematician Hardy that Ramanujan became the scholar we know him as today.

9. INDIRA GANDHI AND PUPUL JAYAKAR

Pupul Jayakar was an Indian cultural activist and writer. She was best known for her work on the revival of traditional and village arts, handlooms, and handicrafts in post-independence India. According to The New York Times, she was known as *India's czarina of culture.* She founded an arts festival that promoted Indian arts in France, Japan, and the United States.

She was friends with 3 Prime Ministers of India: Jawaharlal Nehru, his daughter, Indira Gandhi, and her son, Rajiv Gandhi, and she was a close friend of Indira Gandhi.

Jayakar and Indira Gandhi knew each other since the 1930s. They were growing up together in Allahabad. Pupul Jayakar became a close friend and confidante of Indira Gandhi in her 50s. They remained friends until their last breath.

It was Indira Gandhi who asked Jayakar to write her biography, and Jayakar wrote the book Indira Gandhi: An Intimate Biography in 1992 as she wished.

In her foreword to the book, Pupul Jayakar writes: "This is not a political biography, but Indira's life was part of the unfolding history of India, intricately woven with India's past and future. It becomes inevitable, therefore, that politics forms a backdrop to her public and often private actions. The book seeks clues to her life through access to the many personalities that lay hidden within her. And, if possible, to uncover and reveal Indira Gandhi's thoughts and feelings, her hates and prejudices, her insights and her ignorance, and her loves and the emotional entanglements that generated action."

In her biography, Pupul Jayakar has written about the conversation she had with Indira Gandhi. She writes, *"It was in August 1982, in the middle of the monsoon, that I met Indira on her return from her trip abroad. She was in her study, had shut off her air-conditioners, and opened the windows to let in her garden of verdant green foliage, each leaf iridescent with falling rain."*

"Indira was deeply troubled. Her eyes had started to twitch, and I could see that there was a much deeper depression within her. I asked her whether she was troubled about something."

"For the past month," she said, "I have not slept… I feel a great uneasiness, a sense of foreboding between 2 and 3 in the morning. Night after night, I dream of a venomous old woman, full of hatred, reaching out to destroy me. I lie paralysed, unable to move. But a beautiful human being with a beard protects me and will not let the old woman near."

"Can you go back to sleep?" I asked.

"The moment I close my eyes, the woman is there. I have been receiving secret reports of tantric rituals and black magic rites being performed to destroy me and my sanity."

I let her speak and did not interrupt. When she was quiet, I went and sat next to her.

"Over the years, you have suffered great sorrow. From your childhood, you have pushed all your hate, your anger, and your sorrows into crevices within you, covering them over, never letting them come into the open. Can the surfacing of these dark presences be mind-born, moving out from within to return in the form of dream and dread?"

"Do you accept that there are malignant forces that can be released through tantric rites?"

"Possibly. Even if true, why do you react? You only strengthen these dark forces."

"Do I disregard all the reports I receive every day? What do I do?" There was a touch of desperation in her voice…

"Do you remember, Pupul," she asked me when I went to meet her on October 26, 1984, "that ancient Chinar tree in Beejbihara? I have just heard that it has died." She spoke as if she were referring to an old friend.

Once again, Indira said, «A feeling is arising in me. Why am I here? I feel I have been here long enough.» I had rarely seen her in such a mood, her thoughts entangled with death.

"Once again," she said, "a feeling is arising in me. Why am I here?" And now, "I feel I have been here long enough." I had rarely seen her in such a

mood, her thoughts entangled with death. "Papu used to love rivers, but I am a daughter of the mountains, and my heart is free of care.

I have told my sons (for an instant, she appeared to forget that Sanjay was dead) that when I die, to scatter my ashes over the Himalayas." It was a strange remark, strangely made. "Why do you speak of death?" I asked. "Isn't it inevitable?" she replied."

Jayakar was the only qualified person to write the book because she knew the private memories and the complexes that imparted to Indira Gandhi's public life. Jayakar says, "She was prepared not only to help me but to spend time with me to enable me to understand the contradictions that made her life so complex and obscure."

Jayakar began writing the biography of Indira Gandhi only on the eve of Mrs. Gandhi's assassination. She revealed that her close friend, Indira Gandhi, had personally expressed to her a premonition of her death in the wake of the Operation Blue Star incident.

10. QUEEN VICTORIA AND ABDUL KARIM

Queen Victoria was friends with her Indian servant, Abdul Karim. It was considered an unusual friendship by many.

Their friendship began in 1887. Karim was the queen's teacher who taught her Urdu language. He also educated her on Indian affairs. Much to the resentment of the royal family, the queen showered him with gifts, titles, and honours.

Karim was born in a large family near Jhansi. His father, Haji Wuzeeruddin, was a hospital assistant, which was a good job in those days. He was paid well, so he appointed a Muslim scholar to tutor his son. He taught Karim Persian and Urdu. Karim secured a clerical job at a jail in Agra, and it was there that he was handpicked to serve Queen Victoria in London. He was taught the English language and palace etiquette before he departed for London.

Queen Victoria's first impression of Karim was recorded in her diaries as "tall with a fine, serious countenance." In the Queen's summer home on the Isle of Wight, Karim continued to impress her with delicious recipes. He cooked chicken curry using the spices he brought from Agra. A. N. Wilson, the biographer of Queen Victoria, writes that the dishes were declared "excellent" by the queen, and he was asked to add it to her regular menu rotation.

The queen learnt Urdu from Karim. Urdu was known as Hindustani at that time. She wrote in her diary, "Am learning a few words of Hindustani to speak to my servants. It is of great interest to me, both the language and the people." She was a fast learner. Within 2 months, she was able to write to Karim on her own without having to send messages through other servants. She bestowed upon him the title of Munshi Hafiz Abdul Karim. She made him her official Indian clerk and relieved him of other menial duties.

For Queen Victoria, Karim was a good friend. She signed letters to Karim as "your closest friend" and "your loving mother." She allowed him to bring his wife to England, and she even hosted his father and other family members in the palace. Such special favours given to Karim earned hatred from other Victorian courtiers.

The queen was well aware of this hatred towards Karim. She said it is a "rare prejudice," and the Victorians are simply jealous of poor Munshi. She knew that he would not receive the same respect after her death, so she wrote in her final wishes that Karim would be one of the principal mourners at her funeral. This was an honour given only to the monarch's closest family and friends.

Like she presumed, her family did not allow Karim to stay in London after the queen's death. They sent him back to India and completely erased the Munshi from London's public record. But they could not destroy Karim's personal diary. Even after Karim's death in 1909, his diary was kept alive in the family of Karim's nephew, Abdul Rashid. It was secretly guarded for generations and handed to Sharbani Basu in 2010. She wrote a book on the friendship story of Karim and Queen Victoria. The book was called ***Victoria and Abdul: The True Story of the Queen's Closest Confidante***. Based on her book, she also produced a feature film called ***Victoria & Abdul*** in 2017.

Chapter VIII

FRIENDSHIP IN LITERATURE

FRIENDSHIP IN TAMIL LITERATURE:

Friendship is not just a relationship that is a part of our lives. Friendship is life. Friendship is what makes us who we are. Many literary authors, who have understood what friendship is and how friendship can impact our lives, have written a great deal about friendship in their literary works because they have found it to be one of the essentials a human needs to survive in their lives.

One such remarkable and renowned Tamil poet, Tiruvallur, has written a chapter exclusively on friendship in **Thirukkural**. Thirukkural means 'sacred verse.' It contains 133 chapters, each comprised of 10 couplets. Each chapter talks about the virtues every person must possess in life. This literary work, which has a collection of 1330 verses, has been translated into more than 86 languages around the world.

Tiruvallur, who is the "divine poet" in Tamil literature, has dedicated the 79th chapter to friendship, which is the incredible relationship of life. From Kural 781 to 790, he describes the essence of friendship as follows:

781, *seyarkariya yaavuLa natpin adhupoal.*

Vinaikkariya yaavuLa kaappu.

Tiruvallur is asking a rhetorical question here, asking, "What is better than making friends? What better protection can there be for accomplishing a task?" Friendship is a rare treasure in the world. If one could attain friendship that easily, he could attain anything in this world without any difficulty, is what he means.

782, *nirainheera neeravar kaenmai piraimadhip*

Pinneera paedhaiyaar natpu.

The friendship of the wise waxes like the new moon. The wise people know how to protect their friendship, unlike the fools, whose friendship wanes like a full moon.

783. *navildhorum noolnhayam poalum payildho Rum*

Panpudai yaalar thodarpu.

A good book helps us grow whenever we read it. A reader can enjoy reading a book and get wisdom from it. A good friendship is like a good book; it will give us joy and also nurture us to be better human beings.

784. *nakudhar poruttandru nattal mikudhikkan*

maersenaru itiththar poruttu.

This Kural says friendship is not only for mere fun but also to admonish a friend who makes mistakes in life.

785. *punarchchi pazhakudhal vaendaa, unarchchidhaan*

natpaang kizhamai tharum.

It is not necessary to be next to our friends all the time. Friendship is not about being physically present, but it is about sharing feelings and understanding each other, says Tiruvallur.

786, *mukanhaka natpadhu natpandru nenjaththu*

akanhaka natpadhu, natpu

A good friendship does not only bring a smile to the face of a friend. Friendship is not just a smile on the face, but it is bringing a smile to the heart of a friend.

787, *azhivi navainheekki aaruyththu azhivin-kan*

allal uzhappadhaam, natpu

This Kural explains what true friendship is. A friendship that turns us away from evil ways and makes us walk on the right path is called true friendship. True friendship never leaves us in loss or distress but shares the loss together.

788, *udukkai izhandhavan kaipoala aangae.*

Iddukan kalaivadhaam, natpu.

True friendship hastens to rescue the friend in affliction, like the hand which moves reflexively to secure the loose garment that slips down.

789. *natpiRku veetrirukkai yaadhenin kotpindri.*

Ollumvaai oondrum nilai.

The glory of friendship is said to be on its throne when it possesses the power of supporting a friend in all circumstances.

790, *inaiyar ivaremakku innamyaam endru.*

punaiyinum, pullennum natpu

The lustre of one's friendship will fade off when a friend boasts, "He means so much to me, and I to him." Boasting in such a manner merely demeans a friendship.

The great poet Tiruvallur's ideas about friendship are practical and simple. There are a few more references in history that depict extraordinary friendships that have occurred in the world of literature.

The friendship between King Pari and Kabilar, the great poet, is such an extraordinary friendship.

Kabilar was one of the greatest Tamil poets in the 3rd century BC. He was born in Thiruvadhavur in Tamil Nādu. He has written many poems, including **Inna Narpathu** in **Padhinen Keezh Kanakku Noolgal.** He has also written **Thiruvalluva Malai,** a poem that is a tribute to the legendary poet Tiruvallur.

Kabilar was a good friend to King Pari, who ruled the Velir Kulam. He had a huge love and respect for Pari. Pari was a king of valour. He protected his people like a lion protects its cubs. No enemies could get into his kingdom, which was surrounded by mountains and forests. His kingdom was abundant in all rare treasures one could ever see or hear of.

The strong and mighty Pari was kind-hearted, too. His kindness and love for his people reached Kabilar's ears, and he wanted to meet him in person. So, he went to the king's place and stayed with him for years. Kabilar was in awe when he saw how kind and virtuous Pari was. While in Pari's place, Kabilar took the responsibility to tutor his 2 daughters, Angavai and Sangavai. He taught them Tamil and literature. Pari and Kabilar soon became good friends.

When the praises about Pari spread around, the 3 great Tamil Kings – Cheran, Chozhan, and Pandyan – decided to invade Pari's Kingdom. Kabilar, the poet who knew all 3 kings, appealed to them to stop their invasion. He stood for his friend Pari, but the kings did not pay heed to him. They killed Pari by treachery.

Kabilar lamented his friend's death and sang songs about how great a king he was. He took responsibility for his 2 daughters and tried to marry them off before his life ended. However, he failed to find suitable grooms for the girls. Therefore, he left them in the care of the 'Andhanars.'

Pari's death affected Kabilar. Losing his friend was unbearable to him, so he committed suicide by Vadakkiruthal. It is an ancient method of dying. The one who decides to give his life would sit facing the north and starve themselves to death. It is still practised by Buddhist monks. Kabilar sat facing the north and starved until his death. He died by sitting on top of a rock. The rock is still in place and is known as Kabilar Kundru.

The songs from 105 to 120 and the songs 200, 201, 202, and 236 in Purananooru reveal the love and respect Kabilar had for King Pari.

Another example of an extraordinary friendship happened between Kopperuncholan and Pisiranthaiyar. About 2000 years ago in South India, these 2 friends showed the world what true friendship means.

Kopperuncholan was an early Chola King (100 BC - 100 AD) who ruled from his capital, Uraiyur, which is present-day Trichy. Pisiranthaiyar was a poet from the neighbouring Pandya Kingdom. They never met each other in their lifetime, but they did share a great deal of affection for one another. The king was fascinated by Pisiranthaiyar's poetry. The poet was hugely impressed by the king's governance.

When everything was going fine, and the king's fame and glory were on the rise, a turn of events led to an unfortunate end. The king had some serious disagreements with his 2 young sons because they wanted to rule the country while their father was already on the throne. So, they raised an army against their father. Kopperuncholan could not wage war against his own sons and kill them. Then, the country would be left without an heir. On the other hand, if he gets defeated by his own sons, it would be an unbearable shame to the king.

Therefore, in order to avoid killing his sons or having his sons take over his throne, he decided to die via Vadakkiuruthal. It is an act of shedding one's life without food or water by sitting in a spot facing north. The King was so sure of his friendship that he fixed a spot for Pisiranthaiyar as well next to him and sent word through his men. The people who saw this wondered how Pisiranthaiyar could join his friend from the distant kingdom. His men came back to tell the king that he might come, but it would take so many days for him to arrive from afar. To this, the king replies (excerpt from Purananooru, song 215).

"… in the southern land of the Pandyan king, where they say Pisiron lives. I cannot die without him. He may have stayed away in good times, but he will not fail me now."

As expected, Pisiranthaiyar was late and arrived only after the King passed away. Nevertheless, he sat in the spot allocated for him by his friend, the King, and shed his life just like his dear friend did.

This is such an incredible story of true friendship. Kopperuncholan and Pisiranthaiyar did not even meet when they were full of life. They came together not to enjoy and celebrate their friendship but to end their lives together. Friendship is thus a word for an extraordinary and holy connection of the most sustaining, life-giving, death-defying relationships ever experienced.

Mahakavi Bharathi, the pioneer of modern Tamil poetry, also had many good friends. He was a social reformer and an Indian independence activist. During the times when India was facing many problems under British rule, Bharathi and his friends - Paul, Jayaram Naidu, S. Duraisamy Iyer, V. Chakkarai Chettiar, and C. S. Rangunatha Rao - used to meet regularly in the High Court bench in Madras to discuss the activities needed for our country's independence.

Bharathi had friends in Pondicherry too. They admired him and helped him in his adversaries. Bharathi influenced his friends through his writings and fight for Indian independence. Some of his friends became characters in his poems. Bharathi was close to his friends, so he even called them all by nickname.

He named his house owner Vilakkennai (castor oil) Chettiar, whose original name is Sabapati Chettiar. He named him so because he was as smooth as castor oil in being flexible with the house rent that Bharathi had to pay. Instead of collecting the rent, he would sit for hours listening to Bharathi's poems. Getting immense pleasure by listening to them, he would leave without asking for money. There were other friends who were named 'Vellachu' (jaggery piece) Krishnasamy Chettiar, 'Elikkunju' (mouse) Arumugam Chettiar, 'Valluru' (kite) Naicker, and 'Brahmaraya Iyer' (Professor Subramania Iyer). The nicknames they got from Bharathi were humorous but partly true to what their personality is.

Bharathi conducted research on the Vedas with his friend Sri Aurobindo. His disciples Kanaga Subburathinam (Bharathidasan), Va. Ra. (Va. Ramasamy Iyengar), Kuvalai Kannan, and a great many other loyal friends.

Speaking of his disciples, Chellamma, the wife of Bharathi, has written in her book Bharatiyar Charithiram, "There were about 35 disciples (sishya kodikal) in the house… Each one was different in his own particular way." Among all his friends, Bharathidasan held a special place in Bharathi's heart.

Bharathidasan had immense love and respect for Bharathi and adopted his name as his own name.

Recently, a letter written by Chellama was discovered. It was written to Congressman Kamu Reddiyar from Vadhalakarai near Vilathikulam, who was helping the family with supplies. This letter reveals how the family of Bharathi suffered after the poet's death. Chellama has written this letter without being aware of the death of Mr. Kamu Reddy.

M.S. Sekar, an ex-serviceman and classmate of Mr Pappuraj Reddiyar (son of Mr Kamu Reddy), has a copy of this letter. The letter was posted in the year 1954. It reads, "You promised Koolam (produce) and viragu (firewood). They have not arrived, and I am expecting them. Do not forget and send them. Please bring your children too; I am keen to see them." This shows how difficult the situation was in the poet's house.

M. S. Sekar speaks highly of Bharathi because he was the one who accommodated him in his house when he joined Raja's High School in Ettayapuram.

These anecdotes show how good Bharathi and his friends were. Supporting a friend and helping him with his needs is what true friendship is, and our Tamil literary authors and poets were no less in that.

FRIENDSHIP IN GREEK LITERATURE:

Greek mythology also speaks a great deal about friendship. *Philoi* is the Greek word for 'friend.' This type of friendship is deeply rooted in reciprocity. Exchanging values and support with a great sense of commitment is what Greeks look for in a friendship. For them, friendship is loyalty. They treat the one who is honest and loyal to them as a dear friend.

Achilles and Patroclus were the 2 friends in Homer's epic poem, ***The Iliad***. They were very close to one another. Achilles, the son of the sea goddess, who was stronger than him, acted gentler around Patroclus. They were fighting together in the great Trojan War.

Achilles was heartbroken when Patroclus died in the war. When Achilles refused to fight to protect his honour, Patroclus decided to dress up in Achilles' armour and went out to the battlefield. The Prince of Troy, Hector, thinking of him as Achilles, killed Patroclus. Once Achilles found out about his friend's death, he erupted with rage and murdered Hector.

Achilles knew very well that this act would bring about his own fated death, but he was not afraid of dying. Being heartbroken over his friend's death, he still carried it out. Achilles' strong reaction to Patroclus' death is a sign of their deep friendship. Achilles loved Patroclus as his own; their relationship was possibly deeper than it may seem at first glance. It is written in Book 18 of Homer's ***Iliad*** that Achilles says he loved Patroclus as his own life. Even Patroclus requested that their bones be buried together, which indicates the strength of their friendship bond.

There were another pair of celebrated friends in Greek legend. They were known for their true friendship and sacrifice. They were called Damon and Phythias. They lived in Syracuse, an important part of Sicily. They were very good friends who hardly ever saw each other: 2 young men called Damon and Pythias.

Phythias ran into trouble with a tyrant called Dionysius and ended up in prison. Dionysius condemned Pythias to die in a few days. When Damon heard of Phythias' punishment, he pleaded with the tyrant to release him, but in vain.

Phythias had an old mother and an unmarried sister back home. Before dying, he wanted to bid goodbye to them. When he spoke with his friend Damon, he said he would die peacefully if only he could take care of his mother and sister.

In order to gratify his friend's last wish, Damon went to the tyrant and proposed to take the place of Pythias in prison until he returned from home. He said he would even die for his friend if he did not return from his duty on time.

Dionysius, the tyrant, was surprised that anybody should make such an offer. He, at last, agreed to let Pythias go and gave orders that the young man Damon should be shut up in prison, with a warning that if Pythias were not back in time, Damon would have to die instead.

Phythias promised Damon that he would be back in a few days to release him. He rushed home, took care of his responsibilities, bid his mother farewell, and set out to return to Syracuse.

But on the way back to prison, he was caught up by thieves who tied him to a tree. After struggling for a long time, he managed to wrench himself free and sped along on his way. But then, on the way, he had to cross a torrent. With no second thought, he plunged into the water, fought the waves successfully and reached the shore. He sped fast, for he knew that his friend would die if he were not in Syracuse by sunset.

The last hour came. The guards led Damon to the place of crucifixion, where he sincerely hoped Pythias would come too late so that he might die in his stead. Just as the guards were about to nail Damon to the cross, Pythias entered. Running towards Damon, he hugged him and sobbed with relief. Damon, too, began to shed tears of bitter regret.

Phythias was happy because he thought that he had come in time, even though it was at the last moment. The tyrant, touched by seeing this true friendship, forgot his cruelty for once. He felt that men who loved and trusted each other this much should not suffer unjustly. So, he set them both free.

This friendship of Damon and Phythias has become proverbial. Their story has been a favourite with poets and playwrights, and men who were loyal and devoted friends were often compared with Damon and Phythias.

FRIENDSHIP IN ENGLISH LITERATURE:

Friendship played a vital role in the literary works of English literature. William Shakespeare used the term "friend" in his plays to express a wide range of interpersonal relations. He has used different types of friendship as one of the central themes of his plays.

William Shakespeare's **Julius Caesar** was one such play which was written on the theme of friendship. The characters in the play were friends with each other. Some supported their friends, and some friends betrayed the others.

Brutus and Caesar are very different from each other. Brutus was the play's tragic hero. He was a powerful public figure and a dignified military leader, also a loving friend to Caesar.

Julius Caesar was a great Roman general and senator who showed no aspiration for the dictatorship over the Roman republic. He had his own flaws but still a good friend, who was vulnerable and trusted his friends blindly.

Brutus loved his country more than anything else. All he wanted was for Rome to be safe. But Caesar, on the other hand, wanted recognition for every little thing he did. They differed in many ways, and their differences are what made them friends. Caesar saw only the good in Brutus. Once, he said, *"I have not from your eyes that gentleness and show of love as I was wont to have. You bear too stubborn and too strange a hand over your friend who loves you."* Caesar loved the traits that he did not possess and the traits that he hated in himself.

The other friends, especially Cassius, did not want Caesar to be a crowned king. So, he wanted to influence Caesar's close friend Brutus and asked Brutus if he would want Julius Caesar to be crowned king. Brutus replied that even though he loves Caesar, he doesn't want him to be a monarch. The idea of a monarch ruling Rome with absolute power always went against the ideals of the Roman Republic.

Brutus said, *"I would not, Cassius, yet I love him well."* Brutus' love for his country is greater than his love for Caesar.

As planned, Cassius manipulates Brutus because he believes that if Brutus, who is popular among the people, sides with the conspirators, he can make them appear virtuous rather than offensive.

When Brutus, along with the other conspirators, stabbed Caesar 33 times with their swords, Caesar was shocked. He looked up at his friend and uttered one of the most famous and moving lines in literature. He said, *"You too, Brutus? - Then fall, Caesar,"* and died.

To Brutus, killing his friend is seen as a sad but necessary sacrifice for the people. Brutus wanted to bring peace, which was needed within the

Roman Empire because people were in confusion and chaos when they started to realise that Julius was going to destroy the empire if he wasn't stopped or at least killed. During Caesar's funeral, Brutus stated, *"Not that I loved Caesar less, but that I loved Rome more."* His words made it clear that Brutus was justified in killing Caesar because his intentions were good.

Though the play **Julius Caesar** displays the definition of friendship as a state of mutual trust and support, it also talks about manipulative and betraying friendships. In this play, friendship is the element that sealed the fate of Julius Caesar. We can see that Brutus used the power of friendship to betray him and blind him against the truth. Julius, who was vulnerable to the power of friendship, lost his life because of the conspirators who were in the disguise of friends.

Another one of the most interesting relationships is that of Antonio and Sebastian, which takes place in Shakespeare's **Twelfth Night**. Antonio and Sebastian were good friends who shared a deep friendship. Through the character Antonio, Shakespeare has eloquently expressed the potential of a deep friendship in his play. Antonio, the sea captain, rescued Sebastian from a shipwreck. He then followed him to Illyria, where he was arrested for his former attacks on Illyrian ships. When he was challenged by the Duke, Antonio explained that after he saved Sebastian's life, he also granted the younger man his love and dedication. He was willing to sacrifice his own life for Sebastian.

His words are, *"My love without retention or restraint, All his in dedication."* Even though Antonio knew that entering the territory of his enemy would put him at life-threatening risk, he entered Illyria for his friend Sebastian's sake. In Act 5, he said, *"for his sake ... pure for his love."*

In the play, **Hamlet**, Hamlet and Horatio are ardent friends. Horatio is Hamlet's true ally, and he stands by his friend Hamlet in all his troubles. He even offered to commit suicide for Hamlet.

Helena and Hermia, in the play A Midsummer Night's Dream, possessed a strong friendship until they fell in love with Lysander and Demetrius. Their friendship was separated by the intrusion of these 2 men, but until then, they remained loyal to each other. Helena's selfishness and jealousy caused her to view Hermia's confidence as a betrayal. Their friendship dissolved slowly when they started to fail to respect each other.

In the play **Othello**, Shakespeare created Iago to warn about the dangers of a false friend. Iago makes friends with Othello to take revenge on him. He deceives Othello into trusting him as a supportive friend, but his plan is to destroy Othello with flattery and lies.

In the play **Macbeth**, Banquo is Macbeth's good friend. He was the one who pointed Macbeth towards the spiritual path. Throughout the play, Macbeth is drawn deeper into evil, but Banquo stands by him to bring him towards goodness. Like a good friend, he exhibited loyalty and selflessness to hold Macbeth accountable and support him despite his dark tendencies.

In all his plays, William Shakespeare crafted different kinds of friendships. He portrayed the good friendships and also the bad ones, which could destroy one's life. Shakespeare valued respect, loyalty, and support in friendship, and through his plays, he made the readers understand what true friendship is and how a friendship could impact our lives.

Chapter IX

FRIENDSHIP TODAY

"I don't need a friend who changes when I change and who nods
when I nod; my shadow does that much better."

— Plutarch

The word friend is derived from the Old English source *Frēond*. It is related
to the Old English verb 'frēon,' which means "to love, like, honour, set free
(from slavery or confinement)."

As the word suggests, friendship is love. One cannot say that I do not
love my friend. Friendship is love and also a whole lot of things. Friendship
is built on all the essential things like love, trust, loyalty, and commitment
that are also valued in a romantic relationship. However, friendship is
much better than love because, unlike love, friends come into our lives
without any attachment or feeling. We do not make a conscious effort to
weigh all the elements of compatibility when we make friends. Friendship
happens in our lives with an innate sense that springs from our hearts and
stays there forever.

Friendship has been in the world since time immemorial. Before 2
million years ago, humans were hunters and gatherers. They collected tools
and food and brought them to their favoured spots to sit and eat together.
They shared vital resources with other members of the group, which led
to stronger social bonds and enhanced their chances of survival. They
protected each other from the predators.

During the first half of the 20th century, when World War I and II happened, friendship became an essential relationship to maintain both physical and mental health. Nurses who were tending to the wounded soldiers stayed together and maintained close friendships with each other. Their friendships were formed in an unfamiliar world in which they needed someone who could be a buffer and an anchor. They fondly called each other "pals" and wrote to each other if they were transferred to some other war camp. Because the nurses were cut off from their own people at home, they longed for love and moral support. The comfort and companionship of friendships were like a rock on which they could depend in the darkest times of war. They wrote letters to their friends and about their friendships in their diaries. Olive Haynes, who was an army nurse, wrote in her diary in 1915:

"It's horribly lonely; everyone seems to have each other,"

Wartime friendships were incredibly heart-warming tales. One famous tale was about the friendship between Max Gendelman and Karl Kirschner. Their friendship began during the Battle of the Bulge (1944-1945), which was the last major German offensive campaign during World War II. Gendelman, who was born in Milwaukee and raised as a devout Jew, was captured by the Germans. He tried to escape twice but was caught again and sent to a camp in Lind. Since he was fluent in the German language, he was appointed as the unofficial liaison between the prisoners and their captors.

Kirschner was hiding from his unit on a farm beside the camp. He met Gendelman and became friends with him. He taught Gendelman how to evade the guards and made him come for coffee and a game of chess. This was going on for a while, and on one such meeting, they planned and implemented their escape from Nazi Germany. Kirschner disguised himself as a German and helped Gendelman and another American prisoner pedal their way through enemy lines. Eventually, Gendelman reached American lines and, without forgetting his friend's kindness, helped him move and settle in the U.S. They were good friends for the rest of their lives. Thus, friendship managed to survive even during such bloody battles.

In the 20th century, handwritten letters became the communication tool between friends. When a friend went out of town, the separation became miserable, and letters were written on a daily basis to stay connected with each other. Sharing life events and happenings between friends kept them together, even when they were miles apart. Even strangers liked to become friends, and by writing to them via postal mail, they got to know more about each other and learnt about each other's countries and lifestyles. They were called *pen pals* or *pen friends*.

The Russian empress Catherine the Great and the French philosopher Voltaire were famous pen pals. They corresponded for 15 years until the death of Voltaire. Though they never met in person, they became firm friends and mutual admirers. Voltaire called Catherine "The Star of the North" and the "Semiramis of Russia," in a reference to a legendary Queen of Babylon.

The letters are dated from 1768 to 1777, and in some of them, Voltaire signed himself off as 'The old hermit' or 'V.' In their letters, the 2 friends discussed Catherine's foreign policy and her first war with the Ottoman Empire in 1768-1774. Twenty-six letters from these friends were expected to be sold at Sotheby's auction in Paris. However, they became the object of a fierce bidding war between a mystery buyer and a Russian businessman. The content of the 26 letters has never been published, and the remaining letters between Catherine the Great and Voltaire are stored in the state archive in Moscow and in the National Library in Paris.

One of the other famous pen pals were Elizabeth Bishop and Robert Lowell. They were both famous poets. They were introduced to each other in New York in 1947 by the poet and critic Randall Jarell. Lowell had just published his second book of poems, "Lord Weary's Castle," and Elizabeth Bishop had published her first book, "North and South." Since their first meeting, they corresponded through letters and remained good friends until Lowell's death in 1977. Bishop was a shy woman, unlike Lowell, who was voluble. Despite their contrasting temperaments, they bonded over poetry. They grew close by writing letters to bridge the physical distance between them. Their letters were collected and published in 2008, titled

"Words in Air: The Complete Correspondence Between Elizabeth Bishop and Robert Lowell," edited by Thomas Trevisano and Saskia Hamilton.

In 2019, The Times of India published an article on pen pals who had been writing to each other for 50 years. They are Sunu Kurian and Anne Boyton. Sunu's father was in government service, and they sent a list of the names of government employees' children to the Indian Embassy in Australia in those days for pen pals.

"Anne's school got my name. One day, out of the blue, I got a letter from Anne. I was so surprised and sent her a reply out of curiosity. Then came the second letter, and so it continued for the past 5 decades," Sunu recollected. Through their initial letters, they got to know each other and shared basic information about food, travel, culture, etc. Collecting stamps was their common interest, and that helped them bond well. They sent cards for Christmas and Easter along with letters.

The penfriends also sent pictures to each other. "The first picture she sent to me was of her standing beside her dad's yacht. The last time she sent me her pictures was 18 years ago, saying, 'Sunu, I am putting on a lot of weight, and I am not going to send you my pictures anymore.' Since then, I had no clue about how she looked, and that was my biggest concern while waiting to see her," Sunu said.

The 50-year-old pen pals met each other for the first time at Ferry Wharf F4, Circular Quay in Sydney. When they met, they hugged for a while as if they never wanted to let go. 'It was an embrace 50 years in the making,' said Sunu.

The pen pals still continue writing letters as they believe that no modern communication can replace the joy of writing. Glad to know that such pen pals' culture is still in vogue, despite the expansion of the internet.

One cannot brush off the fact that there is a decline in friendship in these digital times. We cannot dismiss it as a change that has happened because of the growth in technology. Apparently, the meaning of true friendship has taken a toll in the digital world, for a friend is no longer a noun but has become a verb in this age of centennials. "Friend me on Facebook or Instagram" is the conversation starter between people who like to be friends, and unfriending "friends" is not at all considered impolite. If doing so gives us peace of mind and helps us move on to better things, it is absolutely acceptable.

Not all internet friendships turn out bad to take away our peace of mind. Some internet friendships have proved to be good too. Without meeting in person, we still can make friends from different countries. It has its own perks, like learning a new language, sharing our experiences, and talking about our cultures.

The internet has countless possibilities to build oneself. Likewise, good friendships that begin online can also provide equal love and support as real-life friendships. Unlike real-life friendships, online friends can stay in touch 24/7. Meeting people with similar interests is also a piece of cake on the internet. With just a hashtag, one could find persons with similar interests and passions and make friends with them. Surrounding oneself with people who have similar interests will help one grow and achieve goals.

Also, in virtual communities, being vulnerable is easier compared to talking in person. The anonymity in the online presence enables people to feel more comfortable sharing their problems with others. It will help them connect on a deeper emotional level. The introverts who find it difficult to talk with others in person find it easier to make friends online. Introverts always look for like-minded people. Also, they worry about getting rejected because awkwardness happens during interactions. The process of making friendships can be challenging for them. But on the internet, making friends will be less tiring because they do not have to make a physical impression. By showing a glimpse of their inner introverted world, they can be themselves. They can be vulnerable, and those who understand their world will eventually become their friends.

In 2020, when social distancing happened, both introverts and extroverts were forced to socialise online. 'Pandemic survival buddies' were formed. People grew close to those they had never connected with before. "*Frientimacy*" author Shasta Nelson says, "Many of us got closer to fewer people, which is interesting because when we are lonely, it's not that we need to go deeper with a few and feel more seen." Long-distance friends have been able to grow closer, and trying to be a good, compassionate friend has become an important aspect of our post-pandemic life.

In her book *Frientimacy*, Shasta Nelson talks about the 3 requirements of all healthy friendships: positivity, consistency, and vulnerability. Friendship must bring joy and happiness, not exhaustion or stress. To be a good friend, one must be consistent in staying connected with friends. Only when we connect with friends can we discover new aspects of ourselves? Also, it is through vulnerability that we feel seen and known. We should not feel shy or ashamed to call a friend when in need and say, "I need to talk with you." Just being ourselves with our friends is a relief because a good friend will never judge us for who we truly are. One good friend is worth more than a thousand fake friends.

Nowadays, having many numbers of friends does not matter more than having a few good friends. Gone are the days when friends used to be counted on. Now, they are counted up. A multitude of friends make socialising harder. Along with all the commitments in our hectic lives, we find it difficult to maintain our friendships. One scroll on social media feels like enough socialising for us, and we end up getting caught in the loneliness storm. So, how can one be a good friend to someone and receive friendship in return?

"Don't wait for people to be friendly. Show them how" - *unknown.*

To be a good friend, one has to always be there. The very popular TV series 'Friends' theme song lyrics go like this:

So, no one told you life was going to be this way.

Your job's a joke, you're broke, your love life's DOA.

It's like you're always stuck in second gear when it hasn't been your day, your week, your month, or even your year.

I'll be there for you when the rain starts to pour.

I'll be there for you like I've been there before.

I'll be there for you because you're there for me, too.

Being there for a friend in all circumstances is important. That is what makes a good friend. A true friend always tries their best to cheer us up when we are sad or upset over something. Dr Jessy Warner-Cohen, PhD, a clinical psychologist, says, "Oftentimes as friends, we don't like to see people we care about in distress. But hard times happen to everyone. Recognising that sometimes someone just wants you to be with them and understanding the difficulty of the situation can really go a long way. It's not just telling someone that 'things will get better.' It's really showing up for them, letting them know that you hear what they're saying and that you're truly here for them."

Some people do not have problems making individual friends. Doing one-on-one things with their individual friend is easy, but they find it pretty hard to hang out with a group of friends. Because when it comes to making friends, there's an element of randomness to it. The social circle we are found to be with is not totally under our control. We cannot control who we will meet, or we do not know if they will be interested in becoming friends with us. We can't always create the perfect social circle 'to order.' Friends' groups always take time to come together and solidify because every individual is different and unique. With all their individual differences, a bunch of people may need to hang out together over several months before they really start to think of themselves as a group. But if they hang out together for a long time and stick with each other in all circumstances, it will be a really thick group of friends who can hashtag themselves as squad goals.

So, what is the meaning of squad goals? What is a squad?

Nowadays, a group of friends is called a squad. But "squad" isn't a new word. For hundreds of years, it has been defined as a group of people formed for special purposes. Any team of people is a squad, like a cheerleading squad or artists squad or an army squad. The word "squad" comes from the French esquade, which meant 'a small number of military men detailed for some purpose' in the 1640s. Then, the word became a popular slang in the hip-hop community during the early 2000s, as 'squad' became another word for posse or a regular gang of friends. Rapper Fat Joe led a rap collective known as the Terror squad, while rapper Gucci Mane launched "*Brick squad Records*" in 2007.

Though "squad" has been around for quite a while, we have to thank social media for "squad goals." Simply put, squad goals are aspirations for your own squad or group of friends. The term has thrived as a hashtag on Twitter and other image-centric platforms like Instagram. We can tag our friend's photos with #squad goals. Squad goals are versatile. People nowadays tag a lot of group animal photos with #squad goals, making the tag another reason to coo at cute kittens or puppies.

The American singer and songwriter Taylor Swift has always been a poster child for squad goals. She has always been a champion of female friendships. Her squad includes actresses such as Selena Gomez, Cara Delevingne, Emma Stone, Hailee Steinfeld, and Jaime King, who make up her own squad and often play starring roles in her Instagram and Twitter exploits. Many of the people in the squad have even appeared in Taylor's "Bad Blood" music video, as well as onstage at various stops during her 1989 World Tour.

With many of her female friends, Taylor Swift's friendship is still going steady. One of her constant friends is Selena Gomez, an American singer, actor, and producer. They became friends in 2008, and their friendship is still going strong. In a 2017 interview with KIIS FM UK, Selena Gomez shares about how she and Taylor Swift met. "It was amazing because she was the girl with the big curly hair and all the bracelets and the cowboy boots. And I was definitely up-and-coming, and we just clicked," she said. In another interview, Taylor Swift talked about why her friendship with Gomez was so special. "When your life changes and you become thrust into this really strange whirlwind where what your life is. And your life is commented on, and your life is written about, fictionalised, and all that. Both of us have kind of stuck it out and hung in there through all the different changes we've gone through." She added, "Longevity is something you really can find very precious and rare in friendships." Taylor Swift and Selena Gomez have never stopped publicly supporting each other and are still seen together with their other friends.

According to research, a person has 3 to 5 very close friends, 10 to 15 friends in their circle, and 100 to 150 acquaintances in their social network. However, these numbers can vary according to their individual differences, such as personality, career, environment, and social skills.

According to research, the average person has 3 to 5 very close friends, 10 to 15 people in their circle, and 100 to 150 acquaintances in their social network. Naturally, these numbers can vary widely based on your personality, career, location, and social skills. People do not need to have tonnes of friends to be happy. A few good friends are enough to bring true happiness in life. Even celebrities, about whom we would imagine to have loads of friends, have only a few close friends.

Oprah Winfrey says she has only 3 close friends. The famous singer Selena Gomez says the same. Actor Matthew McConaughey says, "I've got only a few really close friends in the 28 years of acting that I keep up with all the time."

To quote Matshona Dhilwayo, author of **The Art of Winning**, "One friend in a storm is worth more than a thousand friends in the sunshine." Being that one friend in a storm is what we call a good friendship.

Nowadays, friendship is described with slang words. Today's Gen Z people refer to their close friends as follows:

- Dawg: This word refers to a close friend, often specifically referring to a male friend.

- Amigo: This is originally a Spanish word, but people of all countries have started using it to refer to a friend, like in "Me and My Amigos."

- Chum: Chum is a word derived from 'chamber fellow.' This word was used in the 1600s but is still in use among friends.

- Bestie: The short form of 'best friend' is Bestie. This is also a widely used word in the world to refer to close friends.

- Mate: Mate is a word used to refer to a not-very-close friend, like a workplace friend or a neighbour.

- Homie: Short form for a homeboy or homegirl with whom we grew up. The one friend who has always been with us since childhood can be called a 'homie.'

- BFF: this is an acronym for "best friends forever."

These are the popular slang words used among friends.

All the concepts in our world evolve with time. The only concept that remains the same across generations is friendship. Only the terms referring to the concept of friendship have changed, but the basic qualities of friendship, such as honesty, open-mindedness, loyalty, and support, stay the same.

Psychotherapist Rhea Gandhi has conducted a study on friendship among millennials and Gen Z. For Snap Inc.'s second global friendship study, she interviewed 30,000 people across 16 countries, including India. She explains: "Creating strong and secure bonds with friends allows for fun, playfulness, and lasting memories for both Gen Z and millennials." People desire more interpersonal connections in friendships. The age of the internet makes it easy for them to connect and be vulnerable about being themselves.

Though social media has liquified the term 'friend,' which now includes many tenuous associations, including old classmates, acquaintances, and even strangers, it helps people to connect and exchange immediate thoughts, which would never have happened without social media.

A photographer named Tanja Hollander became fascinated with the definition of modern age friendship and decided to meet her Facebook friends to see whether the concept of friendship has evolved over time. To find out the answer to her question, "Am I really friends with all of my FB friends?" she set out to visit all 626 of her Facebook friends at their homes and take formal portraits of them.

She titled this project as *Are You Really My Friend?* She travelled to 43 states, 5 countries, and roughly 150 cities in the pursuit of finding out her 'real' friends.

Nearly 95 percent of her Facebook friends have welcomed her and treated her well. They offered her a meal and sat with her for a portrait. Seventy-four percent of people have even allowed her to stay for the night.

One of her Facebook friends, Amy Munger, who was a designer in Houston, Texas, responded to her message about the project very well, and she invited her to stay for the weekend. She gave Hollander a set of her house keys and told her to make herself at home. This kind gesture of Amy Munger made Hollander realise Facebook friends are not just online entities, but they are also as humane and kind as real-life friends.

Hollander wrote on her Facebook page, "Can you really know somebody if you've never seen their home? To me, when I stated that a friend was someone whose house you knew, someone you had eaten dinner with, but now I've realised that might not be as important to the definition of friendship."

Some of her Facebook friends, Hollander has to unfriend because of their lack of response for the project, even after she tried several times to connect with them. But for Hollander, the journeys to her Facebook friends' homes and the portrait sessions brought her closer to them. Friendship is friendship; with all the trust, companionship, vulnerability, and happiness, friendship is a support system without which humans cannot survive.

One cannot deny the fact that online friendships have their own cons, too. The lack of physical presence and the absence of body language can lead to misunderstandings between friends. Also, it is risky if they do not know who the 'real' person is. The credibility is weak when it comes to online friendships. It takes time to really get to know a person. However, if trust and love are mutual, long-lasting friendships can be formed even on social media. Unless the social media connections turn out to be toxic, they are known to have a beneficial impact on health. The happiness friendship gives is crucial for our mental health. Whether virtual or real, friendship can keep us grounded and help us to 'pull ourselves together.'

Chapter X

CELEBRATING FRIENDSHIP

Life is nothing without friendship

– Cicero

During World War II, the term *"security blanket"* was enlisted into U.S. military jargon. It is especially used to refer to those who keep military information secret. The term implies the maintenance of secrecy. Postwar, it also continues to serve as a word for armed protective security measures. However, the term *"security blanket"* was popularised in 1954 when it was used in the American cartoon strip Peanuts. Its creator, Charles M. Schulz, created the character Linus Van Pelt, who carries around a blanket whenever he needs comfort. That blanket was referred to as a *"security blanket"* because it provides security and comfort when wrapped around. The popularity of the cartoon led many people to credit its creator, Schulz, with coining the term.

In June 1954, the character Linus made an appearance in Schulz's cartoon, holding his blanket securely. In October 1954, the Peanuts character Charlie Brown, wearing his signature zigzag shirt, is also shown with a blanket. When Linus's sister Lucy asks him about the blanket, he says, "It's just the thing to have when you are tired and discouraged. See? You just sort of scrunch your face into it, and right away, you feel secure."

Thus, a security blanket is an object that provides someone with a feeling of safety and comfort when they are in a situation that worries them or makes them feel nervous. To be someone's security blanket is to make them feel secure and comforted. Friends are like security blankets. Just a moment spent with them will give us a comforted and secure feeling, taking away all the anxiety from us. In fact, those who give us such a feeling can only be called 'friends,' and the relationship with friends makes life more beautiful.

Friendship not only makes us feel secure but also motivates us, supports us, inspires us, and provides us with a shoulder to cry on whenever there is a need. If we had to list out every little thing friendship does for us, we would have to write a hundred more pages.

"Friendship isn't a big thing — it's a million little things," says Paulo Coelho.

There are many beautiful stories in the world. Everybody has a story of what friendship has done to them and how it has made their life survivable.

A.P.J. Abdul Kalam, the 11th President of India and the author of the book *Wings of Fire,* had 3 close friends during his school days. They were Ramanadha Sastry, Aravindan, and Sivaprakasan. They all studied together at Rameswaram Elementary School. Even though Kalam left the school to go to Rameswaram for his further studies, he remembered his friends and visited them often. One of his friends, Venkata Subramania Shastri, shared in a TV interview that Kalam took him to Delhi for the swearing-in ceremony of his presidency. Kalam arranged a special carriage on the train for his friends and others from his native place. He also arranged a guest house for all of them to stay. They stayed for more than 10 days, and throughout their stay, Kalam, despite being busy with his new presidency, spent time with them, ensured their stay was pleasant, and socialised with them like any other commoner.

Venkata Subramania Shastri recounted some of the memories penned down by Abdul Kalam in his book *Wings of Fire.* Kalam was a close friend of Venkata Subramania Shastri's brother, Ramanadha Sastry. When speaking of their friendship, Venkata Subramania Shastri said, "To improve faith in philosophy, to live up to the standards, and to uplift people were his aspirations as conveyed to my brother."

Abdul Kalam, being a good friend, did not show any racist or social status differentiation, but he imparted virtues and values to his friends. He remained a good friend until his last breath.

Good friends increase our sense of belonging and purpose. A Panchatantra story explains how crucial it is to have good friends in our lives. The story goes like this:

There was once a beautiful forest teeming with lush green trees, plants, and wildlife. In the forest, there were 4 best friends - a deer, a crow, a rat, and a turtle. They lived happily together, playing and having fun.

One day, a hunter came into the forest and captured the deer, which was lazing under a tree. The deer tried to escape the net, but to no avail. The deer's friends came rushing, hearing the deer's cries for help. They noticed the deer lying motionless, caught under the net, and immediately came up with a plan to help him out.

First, the turtle distracted the hunter. While the hunter was busy looking for the turtle, the crow pretended to peck at the deer as if he were dead. This was just an act so that the hunter would think the deer was dead. In the meantime, the rat chewed up the net. In a matter of minutes, the deer was free, and all the friends escaped.

Thus, good friends help each other, no matter how difficult and dangerous the circumstances are. Good friends possess 3 major qualities - positivity, consistency, and vulnerability, says Shasta Nelson. She is a keynote speaker, author, and leading expert on friendship, who has written a book titled *The Business of Friendship*. In her book, she expands on those 3 major qualities of a good friend.

POSITIVITY:

Positive friendships are just as they sound. Friendships benefit our well-being. Friends make us feel more confident. With good friends around, we will have more energy to do things. Also, friends with positivity are fun to be with. They bring a smile to our faces and make everything seem okay.

CONSISTENCY:

Consistency in friendship is all about being dependable. Good friends are a consistent force of reliability in our lives. Consistency is the behaviour of establishing trust and loyalty. As Brown & Brown put it in 2009, 'trust underpins human social relationships, binding people in anticipation of benevolent, reciprocal interaction, which forms the basis for friendship.' Acting in a consistent way establishes trust, which keeps the bond of friendship stronger. Speaking regularly and sharing our thoughts, opinions, and concerns build consistency among friends.

Vulnerability:

It is important to be vulnerable in friendship. Vulnerability is letting down our barriers, opening our hearts, and showing our friends who we really are. Allowing our friends to see our ups and downs and being honest about what is going on in our life is essential in friendship. Being vulnerable is being open, honest, and raw. Being vulnerable strengthens relationships.

According to Shasta Nelson, Friendship = Positivity + Consistency + Vulnerability. In a podcast with Kara Goldin, Shasta Nelson says, "As you practice those 3 things, you move up the triangle, up to the top of the triangle where we have our closest, best friends who have the highest vulnerability with us, the highest consistency, and the highest express positivity."

The essence of friendship is being there for a friend and helping each other during difficult phases of life. Misty Copeland, an American ballet dancer, said, "Anything is possible when you have the right people there to support you." She is the first American woman to be promoted to principal dancer in the 75-year-old American ballet history. At Essence Festival, she talked about her friendship with the late singer, Prince. She gave credit for her confidence to her dear late friend. She said he was the first person who pushed her artistically to have the freedom to do what was inside her, to deliver that, and classical ballet does not really celebrate that. She also added, "The more I performed with him, the more I learnt about who I wanted to be and what I wanted to do as a person and as an artist, so I will forever credit and thank him for that."

Mary Copeland's true friendship story is proof that friendships boost confidence and help us strive to do things better. Sometimes, the biggest deterrent to accomplishing our goals is thinking that we can't. But friends see the strength in us and give us encouragement to accomplish and achieve success in all endeavours.

There are many other books that talk about friendship and how important it is to have friends in life. Having a group of friends is one of the ways to stay sane and healthy. A friendship group can be of 3 to any number of friends. It depends on the one particular person who has knitted his own friendship group together. Researchers have found that a person usually has about 150 friends. The group of friends talk to, share meals with, and 'rotate' hanging around with each other. Some friends from the group have known each other since childhood, and some have only known each other for a few weeks. As we say, every individual is unique and different; every friend in a friend's group can be unique. Some friends can be loud, some can be shy, some fashionable, some can be optimistic, and some can be the exact opposite of optimism. Let's discuss the few types of friends here. One may find it greatly relatable.

1. ***The loud friend:***

   The loud friend is the core member of every friend group. The loud friend is undoubtedly an extrovert with all the extrovert qualities. They enjoy social settings, thrive around people, and are outgoing and optimistic. They are often described as the life of the party.

2. ***The shy friend:***

   The shy friend is the direct counterpart to the loud one. They are the introverts of the group who are typically described as more reserved. They may engage in a multitude of social activities, but they need some alone time to recharge. They take a little longer to get comfortable. However, the shy friend is an ideal companion for movie nights and small group get-togethers.

3. ***The fashionable friend:***

This person always looks trendy and fashionable. They look effortlessly flawless, and they know what fashion is in vogue. They have styling tips to lend to their friends. We noticed how presentable we had started to dress after this friend entered our friend group.

4. ***The optimistic friend:***

This person might have gone through so much in life but still maintains a sense of optimism and positivity that's simply contagious. They see only the positive side of things. They expect and hope everything will turn out well. Having an optimistic friend in a group is beneficial, for every other conversation is bound to have some inspiring undertone to it that will make us think we can move mountains. They make us want to be a better person and keep us focused. Optimistic friends have a way of making everyone smile. It is a blessing to have such a positive friend within a friend group.

5. ***The crazy friend:***

The crazy friend is the one who pushes us out of our comfort zone. They challenge us and encourage us to experience new things. They make us fearless, and by spending time with them, we will unlock many unexplored zones and hidden abilities within ourselves.

6. ***The gossip friend:***

The gossip friend comes in handy when we have had a stressful day. When we need to vent our heart out, the gossip friend is always happy to listen to our problems, and when we are done with venting out, they always have a piece of advice or a joke to improve our mood. We feel like a weight has been lifted from our shoulders after talking with them.

7. ***The long-term friend:***

In every friend's group, there will be one long-term friend. This friend has known us for years, and sometimes it seems like they know us better than we know ourselves. They know all our flaws and mistakes, but they do not judge us. They love us unconditionally. Such friends are always reliable, and this kind of friend is for life.

The idea of friendship has been around for thousands of years. Since ancient times, friendship has been considered a powerful emotion that has changed the entire meaning of humanity. Friendship has been the central theme of many books and literary works. The great ancient Greek philosopher Aristotle exclaimed, "Man is by nature a social animal; an individual who is unsocial naturally and not accidentally is either beneath our notice or more than human. Society is something that precedes the individual. Anyone who either cannot lead the common life or is so self-sufficient as not to need to, and therefore does not partake of society, is either a beast or a God."

A life without friends is not living but just surviving and coping. Life is to be celebrated with friends. Friendship is also to be celebrated. To honour the concept of friendship and celebrate it, a special day was created back in 1930 by Joyce Hall, the founder of Hallmark Cards, Inc.

For example, we have Valentine's Day, Father's Day, and Mother's Day to celebrate our special loved ones. Friendship Day is assigned exclusively to our friends with whom life itself seems to be a celebration. Initially, Joyce Hall proposed celebrating Friendship Day on 2nd August every year.

Joyce Hall is the founder of Hallmark Cards in the year 1930. When he proposed the idea of celebrating Friendship Day by sending Friendship Day gifts and greeting cards, people did not take it in a healthy spirit as they thought the idea was a commercial gimmick to promote the sales of greeting cards.

Then, to contribute to world peace, happiness, and social harmony, the United Nations General Assembly formally established International Friendship Day on July 30. Since friendship is the only way to promote and uphold a familiar spirit of human solidarity, the United Nations made Friendship Day an official celebration.

SOME FRIENDSHIP DAY FACTS:

- Every nation celebrates Friendship Day on different dates. Nations like Finland, Ecuador, Estonia, Mexico, Venezuela, and the Dominican Republic celebrate Friendship Day on February 14.

- In South Africa, Friendship Day is celebrated on April 16, while Ukrainians celebrate it on June 9.

- The U.S. has declared the entire month of February as Friendship Month.

- The Beatles' song "With a Little Help from My Friends" was released in 1967 to commemorate the 10th anniversary of International Friendship Day.

- In 1998, Winnie the Pooh was declared the official ambassador of Friendship Day by Nane Annan, the wife of Kofi Annan, who was the UN Secretary-General at the time.

- In 1999, in Memphis, Tennessee, the Kappa Delta Sorority put a new spin on Friendship Day by initiating National Women's Friendship Day. It is celebrated on the third Sunday in September to specifically recognise a woman's female friends.

- Studies have shown that friends are a great form of stress relief. When a person has healthy friendships, they are less likely to succumb to illness and disease or, conversely, are more likely to heal faster when they do get sick.

- World Friendship Crusade is an international organisation dedicated to celebrating World Friendship Day every July 30th.

Friendship Day is meant to recognise and celebrate the special friendship bond between people. Planning a dinner with friends, watching fun friendship movies, doing fun activities together, and sending greeting cards to friends who live far away are some ways to celebrate Friendship

Day. Some countries have different customs for celebrating special days. Friends exchange friendship wristbands or bracelets between them to express their affection and love. Giving friends such attention and expressing our feelings towards them is important to keep the relationship intact. The phenomenon of this friendship day is all about showing our love to our friends and communicating with them. So, let's celebrate friends and celebrate our life with them.